I Think I Need to Talk to a Doctor

Jason J. Ventre

iUniverse, Inc.
Bloomington

I Think I Need to Talk to a Doctor

iUniverse books may be ordered through booksellers or by contacting:

iUniverse
1663 Liberty Drive
Bloomington, IN 47403
www.iuniverse.com
1-800-Authors (1-800-288-4677)

Because of the dynamic nature of the Internet, any web addresses or links contained in this book may have changed since publication and may no longer be valid. The views expressed in this work are solely those of the author and do not necessarily reflect the views of the publisher, and the publisher hereby disclaims any responsibility for them.

Any people depicted in stock imagery provided by Thinkstock are models, and such images are being used for illustrative purposes only. Certain stock imagery © Thinkstock.

Cover and interior illustrator credit to Dani Ventre

ISBN: 978-1-4759-0580-9 (sc)
ISBN: 978-1-4759-0579-3 (hc)
ISBN: 978-1-4759-0581-6 (e)

Library of Congress Control Number: 2012906096

Printed in the United States of America

iUniverse rev. date: 03/29/2012

DEDICATION

This book is dedicated to all the people that have made a difficult childhood worth experiencing.

A special thanks to my Grandfather, Ray Interlandi. The belief that you and Darling always had in me gave me the strength to get me this far.

When the last page of this book is turned, it's still only the beginning.

To Jennifer,

From the beginning you've been my biggest fan. You've been my loudest cheerleader. You've been my best friend. Thank you.

To all of my siblings.…..What can I say? There are a lot of you! I couldn't be more proud of the people you've become and the influence each and every one of you have had on me.

Lastly, special and sincere thanks to my parents. James Ventre, Ann Grady, John Grady and Bobbie Ventre. I couldn't have asked for a better group of role models.

CONTENTS

PREFACE

This book has been something that I've wanted to write for a while. I thought it would be appropriate to start by explaining why I'm doing this now. I'm writing this book because of a book. Let me explain ...

My grandmother—code name: Mama Darling—once told me about a guy who wrote a biography detailing his bipolar life. I was diagnosed bipolar, so I immediately found a common interest with the author and ended up reading the book. I thought that he'd had a pretty eventful existence at that point. He wrote about trials and tribulations relating to the mental illness. Some of the stories made me laugh. Some made me cry. Some even made me frown and scrunch my face up with anger, while others made me wonder how a person could be so immature, irresponsible, and self-abused. You're probably wondering who I'm talking about and why I'm talking about this person. Well, for starters ...

This person pulled on the heartstrings of America. How did he accomplish this? How could someone write a book about his life and make the hearts of all the readers involved with his story fall for him? Well, how do politicians get elected? They *lie!*

Ladies, gentlemen, and hopefully children who aren't too small, sit back and relax. My story will not contain lies. Aside from a form of comic relief, I'm not going to even exaggerate the truth. What I will do is share my life with you. It's just that simple.

I want you to experience the highs and lows with me, because I feel that's what life is all about. Without the highs and without the lows, life is just plain. To all those who order cheeseburgers plain, congratulations, but when was the last time you were proud of your burger? When was the last time you ordered it and then jumped up on the nearest table, burger raised in the air, screaming, "*Victory!*"?

Let's face it, you haven't. We all need those proverbial pickles and onions, whether we like them or not, because life is all about more, not less, and certainly not plain.

Now, there are about seven things that I can promise you guys:

1. There will be a shitload of profanity. Expecting me to write about something so personal without swearing is like thinking that a great guys'-night-out is attending a Jonas Brothers concert. Just not gonna happen.
2. I truly believe in grammatical errors, and I prefer to stay away from big words as often as I can. Let's face it, anything more than three or four syllables is downright wrong and should be illegal.
3. I'm not going bald. And no, this is not a receding hairline. I just have a temperamental forehead. Now before you start wondering why the hell I put that one in there, let's go to number four ...
4. During the course of this book, if you read a sentence that makes no sense to you or is *waaaaay* out in left field, just do me a favor and do what just about everyone else in my life does: just nod, smile, and move on to something else before you find yourself understanding *all* of my madness.
5. I am a very proud person and don't particularly enjoy admitting when I'm wrong, but when I see the error in my ways, I'll accept my mistakes. In saying that, there's really nothing wrong with the Jonas Brothers. For that, I'm sorry, boys.

6. These stories are *exactly* the way I remember them. That's not to say that if my mother calls me and says I got it all wrong, then I must have lied. I've just lived a crazy life so far, and what I remember happening is good enough for me, so I hope it is for you.

And lastly ...

7. I am truly sorry to my family and friends for the way that I've lived my life. I don't expect that at the end of this book I will still have your respect, support, or even partial admiration, but to those of you I love as family and to those of you I call my friends, I sincerely thank you for being there for me.

Well ... where do we go from here? Let's talk about my life! I'm confident that at the end of the discussion, you might agree ...
"I think I need to talk to a doctor."

I

WHO AM I?

Hi. My name is Jason Ventre. My friends call me Jase. I was born August 10, 1980. I have brown hair and really blue eyes.

I'm 5 feet 11 13/16 inches tall, but I claim to be 6 feet.

I hope you understand.

At one point, I dated a girl who just *loved* to tell me that I'm not six feet tall. I don't know what her problem was. Usually girls are happy that the guy they are with is at least six feet tall. They are also quite comfortable in their ignorance when he adds a few fractions of an inch, so they can just act like they believe him and not get stuck with a short guy.

As far as my skin type goes, well, I'm Italian, but there's no spot on an application for Italian, so I guess I'm white with a tan complexion. At least I don't say I'm caramel-complected. I never really understood why some people would compare their skin tone to food toppings. Would that make Lindsay Lohan orange sherbet–complected? All I know is, unless the ladies are going to put on the mythical whipped-cream-sundae bikini, they should stay away from the ice-cream topping descriptions; we're not that hungry.

So, getting back on track, my favorite color is green; I think polar bears are really cool; my favorite beer is Sierra Nevada; and I have a high school–equivalency degree.

I meet people all the time who say they have a college education, but my question to them is always this: "What did you learn while you were there?" They usually respond with the exact title of what they received their degree in, like, "Oh, I have a bachelor's degree in computer market research analysis."

Ever wonder about that? Come to think of it, it kind of pisses me off, because one of two things just happened:

1. They found my subpar collegiate résumé to be too unattractive to actually delve into what they learned at college. Maybe they just assume that my puny GED head might explode because I can't handle the transfer of *all* that knowledge.

Or …

2. The only thing they bothered to learn was the title associated with their degree. They memorized it because they didn't want anyone to know that they just wasted a hundred grand of Mommy and Daddy's money and all they have to show for it is an amazing Beer Pong throw.

In the event that either of my suspicions are true, I say to all you brilliant college minds, *"Experientia docet."* That's Latin. Look it up, bitches!

So, I was born in Bristol, Connecticut, to a lovely Italian woman. Her name is Ann, and I was her third child. Things were great until she had five more. We'll get into that later.

❋❋❋

Being the third oldest child in my family, out of eight kids, was kind of cool, except I can't really brag about it. I mean, really—when was the last time the bronze medalist was interviewed and treated like a national hero? Imagine if Michael Phelps won eight bronze medals … what could you even do with bronze? I guess you can melt it down and make a real-life statue of you losing to two other people. Come to think of it, you didn't even come close to winning. You came close to the person who came close to winning. I think they should just get rid of the bronze medal and give that loser a really small pin that says "Thanks for trying; we needed a good laugh. PS: your family called and wanted me to tell you that they moved."

***

My favorite football team is the New York Jets. The first football I ever touched said NEW YORK JETS on it, so I guess it was just predestined. Thanks, Mama Rose. That's my father's mother. I guess she was a Jets fan too. Growing up a Jets fan was pretty easy for me because up until I was fourteen, I lived on the East Coast. I also wasn't nearly as protective about my team as I am now. I find myself getting into arguments with random people to defend the honor of a team I watch on TV once a week.

Case in point: there was this woman—whom we will refer to as Miss Flatchulants—manning the cash register at the local gas station. I was running a little late and only had five minutes to purchase some snacks and tasty beverages before the game came on. I frantically ran into the store searching for a six-pack of Sierra Nevada, located it, grabbed it, and sprinted up to Miss Flatchulants in hopes of a speedy checkout …

Now, there are a few things I feel responsible for trying to teach anyone reading this book. The lesson has only three steps, but to ensure that we take all necessary precautions, I've made a short list:

1. If you see a person who appears to be in a rush and that person is wearing a New York jersey, do not—I repeat— *do not* act like a smart ass. It's just a bad move.
2. If you're a cashier and someone with that jersey comes into your store looking for a quick exit, please don't find

it necessary to take your time. If the barcode won't scan, just type in the damn numbers.

3. The final step—and I can't stress it enough—*DON'T* look at that rushed, anxious New York fan in the eyes and say, "Oh, the Jets? They suck!"

Now, if you're that person who doesn't want to take my advice, go ahead and try these things—see what happens. If you're lucky, like Miss Flatchulants, all you'll hear is "Hmm, is your mother still upset she had you?"

The interesting thing about this particular story is that the gas station cashier didn't get angry; she simply shrugged her shoulders and said, "Yeah, probably."

I smiled at her, wished her a blessed day, and yelled, "Go Jets!"

Hopefully, at this point, you're laughing because you're starting to understand the flow of my personality. Either that or you're wondering where your receipt is and if there's enough gas in your car to get you back to the bookstore. I did warn you with the title of this book that I may need to talk to a doctor, so it's only fair that you keep reading.

❊❊❊

I have small hands and feet. This isn't something that I'm proud to admit, but this chapter is about giving enough information about who I am so you guys out there feel like you know me a little bit before we take this journey together. I'm not saying that I'm built like a freakin' hobbit, but at the same time, I'm no Shaq. I used to hope that one day I'd wake up and they'd be larger and next to me there's a note addressed from God saying, "Sorry about the small hands; we needed a good laugh. Here are your real ones … I bless you. Love, Me."

Until then, this is what I'm working with.

I have nine siblings.

My father (James) and mother had two boys and two girls: (in order) Jamie (boy), Kellie (girl), me, and Dani (girl). Then they got divorced and married other people. My mother and *stepfather* (John) had four more, one girl and three boys: Erin (girl), Jacob, Joshua, and Eli.

My father's second marriage to my stepmother, Bobbie (girl), netted two more sons: Stephen and Lucas.

When my parents got divorced, I was two years old. Dani was still a little baby. Suffice it to say that I don't remember having to deal with any ill feelings toward either side, because of the young age. At that point, there were just four siblings, all about two years apart. I'd be lying to say that I know the exact reason why my parents divorced, and I'm sure that not being clear on that has had some sort of effect on me. On the other hand, I'm sure my parents wanted to protect us, so maybe it's the kind of mystery that I don't want to solve at this point in my life. When I did inquire about it, both sides had two completely different stories, so at this point, who cares? They aren't together, and gas prices are going up again—which do you think is more important?

I was blessed with an amazing set of grandmothers. My father's mother, Mama Rose, is a woman who has always cared about her family, and she's just a delight to be around. Unfortunately for her, my mother had main custody of us, so I can safely say that we probably spent more time with my mother's mother, Mama Darling. I could go on and on about the personal integrity that possessed Mama Rose and explain in great detail about how great a lady she is, but again, this chapter is about getting to know who *I* am and because Mama Darling was just as much of a motherly figure to me as my own mother was, we need to concentrate on her for now. No offense, Mama Rose.

I had really blond hair when I was a young boy. Out of the first batch of four children that my mother had, I was the only one with blond hair and blue eyes. The other three have brown hair and dark—from dark hazel to brown—eyes. Mama Darling was obsessive about the overall maintenance of my hair, growing up. I look back on how she always wanted to make sure that every strand of it was properly styled and *moussed*. I really miss that. Now my hair is brown, and I keep it short, because I realized that when you don't have someone to treat you like royalty like she did, you stop caring.

There was a lot of hype growing up about how handsome a man I was going to turn out to be. I'm not saying that you shouldn't believe the hype, but what no one expected was that I would grow a neck quite like the one I have now. It's a little on the long side, and I've spent most of my life embarrassed about it. About a year ago, I learned how to scrunch it down and hide it a little. It helped my self-esteem out quite a bit. Sometimes I overdo it though, and I go from looking like Geoffrey the Giraffe to Uncle Fester. My father is always trying to teach consistency, I hope to learn that lesson one day.

I've been skinny most of my life. I know, I know: poor me, but seriously, it was horrible. I have an attitude—sometimes backed by a temper—similar to a rabid alligator with a toothache, but the body of a Backstreet Boy. It's such a conflict. It seems that every time I get angry at someone, I have to act even crazier than I normally am just so they'll take me seriously. I know that there's a Small Man Syndrome going on out there, but is it possible to have a Skinny Man Syndrome? If so, then I've definitely got it!

So … my family's heritage makes me 75 percent Italian and 25 percent Irish, but I usually just tell people that I'm Italian. I mean, it just sounds better. Besides, because I don't drink a lot anymore, there's no real point in saying that I'm Irish; is there? I also like to do everything in my power to tell people when I find a really good Italian restaurant. You can't really do that with the Irishness. How would that sound? "Hey, Uncle Patty, there's a really good Irish restaurant down on O'Shannon Way." Besides, the menu would probably only consist of whiskey, potatoes, corn beef and cabbage, and an ad for the time and place of a local AA meeting.

I have an addictive personality to everything, but drugs. It's actually proved to be a dangerous trait to have. At one point, I owned ten different pairs of K-Swiss sneakers. Who needs all those? I now have an understanding of what women go through with shoes, because I will literally spend my biweekly grocery money on them, and then spend the next two weeks eating lunch at the numerous Costco sample tables. It's horrible, and I don't see an end in sight. Now I'm into watches too, and although I can only wear one at a time, I find myself shopping around for them as often as I can.

I once had a roommate who collected colognes. That's not that bad, but the problem was that he wouldn't wear any of it. I guess he just liked the way the bottles looked.

One day I came home from work, and as soon as I walked through the front door, I was met with the normal *entryway funk*. I couldn't take it anymore. I had to do something. This guy was just out of control, and I had to find a way to tell him that I no longer appreciated his scent. I felt bad for what I was about to do, but I didn't have a choice. When he walked in the same door and seemed unfazed as the cloud of invisible nastiness gave him a big welcome home hug, I walked up to him, looked him right in the eyes, took a deep breath, and said … "Hey." That was it; I couldn't do it. I felt bad.

Back to me.

I have a passion for country music. Up until I moved to Arizona, I listened to all kinds of music *except* country. I hated it. I don't know if it was the accents that irritated the hell out of me, or the mullets, or the tight pants, but there was just something about it that I couldn't stand. That hatred turned into an educated passion, which then turned into a desire or maybe even a fantasy to *become* a famous country singer. I'll tell ya, life has twists and turns all the time. One minute, I'm listening to gangsta rap and really feeling my African roots; the next minute, I'm singing about how my wife left me but my cousin is really attractive.

After a couple of tries attempting to make it big in country music, I settled for an unpaid career in the wonderful world of karaoke. As fun as it is, it's still embarrassing to admit and almost an instant deal breaker in trying to meet those really good-looking, successful girls. I have learned that there are two things that you shouldn't mention when describing your hobbies to a girl. One is karate and the other is karaoke. To you, they may be the coolest things in the whole wide world, but for some reason, it's just not considered desirable to the opposite sex.

✳ ✳ ✳

Spiders scare the shit out of me.

I don't know what it is about them, but they are the one thing I don't like that actually give me goose bumps when I see them. I can honestly say that I've never met a spider that I liked. I personally think they're all condescending pricks. All they do is stare at you with all those arms and legs as if you're substandard because you only have two of each. What gives them the right? One spider just the other day came over to me and stood there staring. I looked down at him and said, "What the hell are you looking at?" Without hesitation, he pointed to me eight times and laughed. Asshole.

Most of my fears I face head on—like heights, for example. I'll go on any roller coaster ride knowing that I'm totally scared, but I just don't care. I love life. I think it's precious. My family and I are a little surprised that I'm still here experiencing it. We'll get to those juicy stories soon.

So I was trying to think of a way to end this chapter in hopes that you can't wait to start the next one. I guess I can say this:

I first started running away from home when I was six years old. I've moved more and lived in more states than I care to think about right now. I've been married enough times to understand the quintessential gambler's reasoning: "If I just do it one more time, I'm sure to win …" I fall in love quick, but fall out of love quicker. I joined the Marine Corps on sheer impulse. Made money, lost money, and have gone bankrupt. Served time in jail. Been beat up, dragged out, and left for dead.

And just when you think life shouldn't have to be more challenging, I was diagnosed with bipolar disorder.

Yep, that's me. Just your everyday run of the mill, walking, talking, exaggerated miracle.

PART 1

2

As Far Back as I Can Remember

The first time I overdosed, I was around three and a half years old. I'm not going to say that I was depressed at that young an age and couldn't go on any longer, because let's face it, I had it made. My mother changed my Huggies regularly, and the consequence-driven, vegetable force-feeding didn't happen till later in life; so at the time, things were great.

Looking back on it now, I know that the reason I needed to eat those delicious grape-flavored chewable Tylenols was because they were delicious. What kid doesn't like the flavor, grape? The reason was simple and quite yummy.

I remember sneaking in the kitchen and climbing up on the counter to where my mother kept the stash. I opened the cabinet, and there they were, all wrapped up like tasty little candies. I just had to have some. I can almost picture myself looking around as if I had just broken into someone's house, located the safe, and was about to crack it open.

My family has always said that I belong in sales, and that was evident during my initial altercation with the grim reaper, because I had sold my sister Dani on the idea of popping a few of those in her mouth as well. Keep in mind, she was only around two years old at the time.

I can't say that I remember much past that point, except that I did have my stomach pumped. Suffice it to say that ever since I ate all those damn Tylenol's, grape hasn't tasted quite the same, and one of my least favorite colors is purple, which suddenly occurs to me that it might explain my deep-rooted hatred for Barney. I hate that freakin' dinosaur.

The Earlier Years

Dani was the fourth child and the last from my mother's first marriage—with our father. I can say that growing up, she and I were probably the closest of the siblings. I liked playing with her better than our older sister and brother because of the personality dynamic between us compared to the other two. Dani was a tomboy. Actually she still is, but back then, we liked to do the same things together. She always wanted to be one of the boys. Instead of playing house fantasizing about the normal things that kids do, our game consisted of me being the son and her being the father. I used to call her Dad, and she called me Child. Instead of running a household in this game, we ran a construction company—and fixed shit.

I always thought that the game Dani and I played was a normal childhood fantasy game, but looking back on it now, that shit ain't normal. Come to think about it, it might have been a direct reaction to all of the grape Tylenols we'd consumed. Can you sue a company for marketing such a great flavor and jeopardizing the health of young children? I'll have to look into that.

I also enjoyed playing with Dani a lot because my brother, Jamie, never really made sense to me growing up. I can remember when the first Nintendo came out. After the initial Super Mario Brothers craze, he started to play one-player sports games and would hand me the second controller and convince me that I was playing. Of course, it wasn't me playing, but instead it was the computer. I didn't know any better, and he would just sit there without saying a word enjoying his mental victory over an innocent little kid. What a dick!

Naturally, someone bought it for him because he was the first-born child, and I guess I couldn't have one because four-year-old kids aren't smart enough to tackle such intricate technology. Yeah, I'm gonna call bullshit on that one. I know a girl whose four-year-old son invented the Internet and then sold the idea to Al Gore. All right, all right; that's a stretch, but it totally has mental validity. I think kids nowadays are way ahead of where I was back then, and it has everything to do with electronics. I saw a little kid in the grocery store the other day. He had to have been eight years old or so, and he was complaining to his mother that the battery power of his new Smartphone is highly unacceptable. His concern, moving forward, he said, is that when cell phones transfer over to a dual processor and the tech companies don't find a way to increase battery strength, his phone will surely die, leaving him stranded with no e-mail access! Yes, that is what he said! Is that what kids worry about now? And what the hell kinds of e-mail is this kid getting? Whatever happened to the innocent age, when it was okay to worry if your sister would grow up still wanting to be your father?

My older sister, Kellie, was kind of hard to deal with for me, as a young boy growing up, because she was the prissy one in the family and it was difficult for me to relate to her that I have mostly wiped her from my memory of those years.

After my parents split up, my mother moved us kids (Jamie, Kellie, Dani, and me) from Bristol, Connecticut, back to Stamford, where she grew up. My grandfather owned a two-family apartment building, and the five of us lived in the two-bedroom apartment on the first floor. Jamie and I shared a room. Kellie and Dani shared a room and my mother slept on the pullout sofa.

My time in Stamford isn't packed full of memories, but what I do remember is that Mama Darling would come over almost every day to help my mother out, because she was working and going to school. I'm sure you're thinking that any mother would want to help her daughter, but Darling was a freakin' super hero. Not only would she come over and make us breakfast, pack our lunches, and walk us to school, but she did it with *cancer*. Yes, the Big C. And when I tell you she packed our lunches, I mean she put together enough food in that little lunch box to feed all of Kate plus eight kids. And the things that Darling put in those lunches—fuhgeddaboudit! It was a feast!

After school let out, Darling would be out front waiting for us, and would walk us home to a completely spotless house and then babysit for us. I specifically remember her smiling every time I asked her to fix me some cut celery with cream cheese—Philadelphia cream cheese, to be exact. It was as if she just loved to give us what she knew would make us happy. That never changed.

Before my grandfather built a workshop in the backyard, there was a grassy, woodsy area where my siblings and I would go out to play. One day, Jamie and I were in the backyard, and I was playing on one side of the yard and he was off in the distance somewhere. I was minding my own business and eating my celery with cream cheese (you know the kind), when all of a sudden I heard a scream. I turned around, cream-cheesy celery in hand, just in time to get hit in the eye with a hammer.

I'm not going to say that I took it like a champ. The hammer hit me so hard, my celery flew out of my hand, and the mere force knocked the damn cheese right off the cream!

The story I remember was that Jamie saw a hammer on the ground and picked it up. On the hammer was a centipede. At that time, Jamie was afraid of insects, so as a reaction, he threw the hammer. As if caught in a tornado, the hammer spun around over and over again until it got tired and took a nap on my face. I screamed loud enough to break a window, then I hit the ground, and my brother hit the pavement running down the road.

It wasn't before long until the doctors realized there was nothing they could do and recorded the time of death at 4:58 p.m.

Totally kidding! Obviously, I'm not dead!

I'm sure at some point I ran inside screaming and crying hysterically just like the time my transformer broke because it hit my sister in the head and I couldn't play with it anymore. (Who does she think she is to jump head first into *my* transformer and break it like that? I'm still to this day very upset with her about that.)

Focusing back on the story at hand …

I had a black eye that day to match what you would expect to see if Chelsea Handler's friend Chuy picked a fight with Mike Tyson. My mother eventually caught up to my nine-year-old track star of a brother and beat his ass!

I felt really bad about that up until this past Fourth of July, when I confronted my brother about it, refreshing him with my version of the story and then asking him if he remembered.

He said, "Um, yeah, Jase … I don't know how to tell you this, but I wasn't afraid of bugs."

I simply laughed and said "Whatever."

He replied with, "No, think about it: I'm supposedly afraid of insects, so I pick up a hammer off the ground in an open field, and instead of just dropping it, I throw it, and of *all* the places it *could've* gone, it hits your little pea-sized head?

I stood there staring at him for a second. Was I supposed to still have those previous feelings of anger and adrenaline toward my older brother, now, at the age of thirty?

I said, "So, you mean to tell me that you purposely threw the hammer at my eye?" I started to feel a fire building up in my chest.

He said, "Actually, no."

For a second I felt relieved. I'd had a feeling all growing up that the way I remembered the story was probably wrong. It had to be. We were family. We were brothers. We were video game partners (well kind of).

He then smiled and said, "I actually never threw it. I *swung* the hammer, and it hit you in the eye.... Oh, and when you heard a scream, that actually wasn't it at all. That was my *war cry*."

I'm still trying to decide if I should submit that restraining order paperwork.

3

The Introduction and the Finale

I remember the first time I met my stepfather. I was around four years old.I walked into our , and my mother heard me come in. She asked me to come over to the living room. I listened to her, and there sitting on the couch was a gentleman with a really welcoming smile. My mother introduced me to him, so I looked him in the eyes and shook his hand. It was something I had learned to do at a very young age. Eye contact *had* to be made to show respect for the person you were meeting, and the handshake had to be strong to show that you were confident in who you are.

I didn't disappoint my teachers. I shook his hand the right way. I can vividly remember what he looked like as if my brain was instructed to hold that memory up there for some reason. I even remember that he was sitting toward the middle of the couch, which I remember thinking was kind of odd because there's no place to rest your arms in the middle.

What I don't remember is being introduced to any of the other men my mother *may have* dated. I didn't realize until later in life how important that was. I'm hoping that the single mothers in America are paying attention to my clear recollection of that day and come to learn that through the details of what a small child remembers, your dating decisions could do a lot of harm to a young kid.

Now, I couldn't tell you how long they dated for, but eventually there was a wedding and I was invited! I remember feeling very excited to be there. Who wouldn't? I used to love dressing up for special events, and to this day still do, but this was different. How many times can you see your mother get married? (Some of you, please don't answer that.)

At the wedding, my brother Jamie decided that he was going to dare me to get up on the dance floor and "shake my booty." I would of course accept his challenge, because in my mind I was the absolute best break-dancer alive! Nobody could touch my skills.

When a good song came on, one that said, "Hey, Jase, time to go to work," I stood up, gave my brother a wink, and started walking toward the dance floor. On the way over, the lights softly dimmed and a gigantic disco ball slowly lowered its way from the ceiling. The crowd grew quiet and anxious for my performance. They were all on the edge of their seats, because they had been waiting for this day to come for so long. Some of them, if not all of them, had camped out to buy tickets years before the show.

I stood there, all three-plus feet of me, legs apart, head down. My one Michael Jackson glove glistened under the lights from the heavenly ball above me. The music came on, my knee started to bed as my hips started to wiggle. I raised my head slowly and seductively. Making eye contact with all the ladies in the crowd, I could see them intently and anxiously leaning forward. I gave them a quick pelvic thrust and half of them fainted right then and there. I knew I had them. I knew I was the best.

The music played on, and with every passing note, my body became more alive. I was like a crazy dancing gymnast, but with the grace of a seasoned ballerina. I twirled, flipped, and skidded myself across the dance floor refusing to end the show. My fans deserved more. They were loyal. They were mine.

I smiled and closed my eyes, taking in all the glory. I was positive that this is what it felt like to be in heaven. When I opened my eyes, my brother Jamie was staring up at me wondering what the hell I was doing. I hadn't even moved.

He said, "Well, are you going to get up there or not?"

I said, "Yeah, of course."

It was all a dream. I remember feeling very sad and alone. My fans were all gone and replaced with an empty hardwood dance floor. I knew I couldn't back down from the dare, so I walked up to that floor hoping and praying the whole way there that maybe I really was the best dancer alive and my limitless skillset would just show up all of a sudden.

When I got there, I turned toward the audience, sat down on my butt, spun around once, got up, and went back to my seat. I wasn't ready for the spotlight, and when I saw my brother's big grin, I knew he had won. It was one of the saddest days of my young prepubescent life.

4

On the Road Again

With my mother and stepfather's wedding and honeymoon behind them, a decision was made to move back to Bristol, Connecticut, my birthplace. I'm guessing that I didn't have anything against the move, because I don't remember it. I don't remember visiting the house during it's time being built, and I don't remember moving our belongings there. I'm assuming that it was probably difficult to leave my grandparents, but because of the lack of memories for this particular time in my life, I can only assume.

We got settled into our new home, and everything seemed to be okay. I was sharing a room with Jamie, and the girls shared a room down the hall. It was the same setup as what we'd had in Stamford, but my mother and stepfather had their own room. I'm sure they picked that house for sound and responsible reasons, but I'm sure my mother was also excited to be off the couch. That made me happy as well.

Life in a shared room with Jamie was okay, I guess. He certainly wasn't the neatest person to live with, and we would get in trouble because the room would get messy pretty quick. I don't know how many times he made me clean it. He was always making me clean up his mess. I should send him an invoice. He also felt that finding a proper place to dispose of his boogers wasn't necessary and instead painted them on the wall our bunk beds rested against. At one point, it started to resemble a Picasso painting, so you could say I encountered my first experience with abstract art. To make matters worse, my mother noticed the painting and scolded both of us! I tried to deny it by telling her that I slept on the top bunk and there was no way I could have done it. Just when she started to believe me, Jamie said that he wasn't doing it, and put the blame on me!

I couldn't believe it! Of all the lowdown things to do! I had to get him back for his betrayal. That night after dinner, I felt the need to completely hydrate myself. Call it "proper daily liquid consumption"; call it "a search to quench my thirst"; or call it what you want. Personally, I'm gonna refer to it as "the flow for my bro."

I drank and I drank and did everything I could to avoid going to the bathroom, and when it was time for bed, I hopped up on that top bunk like a tiny Chinese acrobat.

My brother crawled into his bottom bunk—that had been freshly cleaned by me, the accused booger thrower—and turned on the radio like he did every night. I lay there waiting for the perfect opportunity to strike. I lay there staring at the ceiling, and when he changed the radio station for the last time and an hour went by, I closed my eyes and relaxed my body. A smile came to my face as I felt the warm sensation of releasing all the water I had collected that day.

As you can imagine, shortly after the release, all hell broke loose. Parents were notified, and he was out to crucify me. I wanted to tell them that I didn't pee on my brother. I wanted to deny everything. I remembered wanting to get back at him for saying that I was the one flinging the boogers, but it wasn't like I could just say to my mother, "Umm, yeah, I didn't pee on him; he peed on himself." I didn't think they would believe my story, so instead I just stood there and cried until everyone stopped yelling. I knew right then and there that I wasn't happy in that household; it was time to go.

The next morning, I was punished and sentenced to hard time in solitary confinement, and I decided to start planning my first official escape. I had to leave. I had to hit the road. Who were these people who were trying to tell me who I could and could not pee on? I needed to come up with a plan. I knew that I would need some money and something to put my valuables in, but even with those items, something was still missing.

As I lay there in bed that night, on my freshly scrubbed mattress and washed sheets, I tried as hard as I could to figure out what I felt wasn't quite right, and just when I was about to give up on it and fall to sleep, it hit me! The only thing I was missing was my little sister, Dani. I needed to take her away from all of this. What eight-year-old boy would let his only little sister stay in an environment like this? I decided to take her along with me. I would take care of her.

The next morning, I woke up really early, probably sometime around 4:00 a.m. I quietly made my way downstairs to the kitchen. I climbed up onto the counter and opened the cabinet. There in front of me were tiny little rolls filled with copper treasure! My mother kept rolls and rolls of pennies up there, and now they were mine! I grabbed a couple of handfuls of them, and as I was about to close the cabinet door, I saw to the right of the pennies, were some chewable grape Tylenols. My whole body shivered, so I growled at them, closed the cabinet door, and climbed down off the counter.

Leaving the rolls of fortune on the counter, I quietly opened the back door and walked outside. I now had enough money to support my sister and me, but I still needed to find a way to carry my things around. Within seconds, I spotted what I was looking for. About ten feet in front of me was the most amazing stick I'd ever seen. It was like it was purposely put there, begging me to pick it up and take it with me. So I did.

Locating a bandana in the house, I turned that stick and bandana into an old-school, highly portable piece of shoulder luggage.

The only thing I needed to do to complete my handy suitcase was to get my most valuable possessions and add them to it before I tied it up. I snuck back up to my room and grabbed my Transformers toys. They were the only things that I needed. As I walked out of the room, I passed my Pet Monster and gave him a hug. I felt bad for leaving him like that, but he was too big for me to carry, and he knew it.

With my Transformers with me, I walked over to my sisters' room and woke up Dani. I told her briefly what was going on and convinced her that she was better off with me.

Surprisingly enough, she got right up and followed me downstairs.

I added the Transformers to my stick bag, along with the pennies, and locked the back door. We were ready to set out on our journey.

Dani and I walked out the front door and made our way up the street to the main road. We had no destination, but we didn't care. We had money, we had Transformers, and we had each other. That's all that mattered.

We marched up the road without saying much to each other at all, and after around three hundred miles or so (which is kiddie-measurement distance of about one mile), we got tired and hungry. Luckily enough, there was a gas station not too far off in the distance, and I knew that they had some type of hearty nutrition that my sister and I would need to build enough strength to continue our journey.

When we got there, we looked around for the most responsible selection as we could find. We selected our items and brought them up to the counter. The clerk scanned: two packs of Skittles, one Starburst, a Milky Way bar, and three packs of watermelon Bubblicious.

We were now ready to eat our first breakfast. Fifteen minutes later, our tummies started to hurt and we were out of money. It was time to go home.

We turned around and started walking back toward home. We didn't want to have to walk that far, but the sugar from our amazing breakfast gave us the energy. About a quarter of a mile or so into our trek back home, a cop car pulled over on the side of the road in front of us and Officer Bernie Fiferman stepped out. He was a tall fellow and equipped with standard-issue police necessities: mirrored sunglasses, a large overly compensated nightstick, a somewhat offensive moustache, and thatodd looking police hat with the shiny bill

He walked over to us a little too fast for my taste, and I didn't appreciate it. I didn't owe this guy money—who did he think he was anyway?

Naturally, the first question out of his mouth was, "Where you kids heading?"

I felt a need to protect my little sister. I threw up my upper lip and, with confidence, said, "We're going home." With that we started walking, and he stopped us again. The nerve of this guy! He asked us if our parents knew where we were right now, and feeling the pressure from the grand inquisition, I said no. With that, he forced us into the backseat of the cop car and drove us home.

When we got there, we walked to the back of the house, and I remembered that I had locked it before I left. Damn! He then got on his radio and called dispatch to have them call my mother. I don't know what they said to her, but a mere couple of minutes later, she opened the back door to see her littlest children standing next to Officer Fiferman. She quickly grabbed us and pulled us into the house and then went back outside to speak with ol' Bern.

I didn't know at the time what they were talking about, but years later my mother told me that the officer was lecturing her on the safety of her kids and kept asking her why she didn't know where we were. She kept telling him that we were eight and six years old. How was she supposed to know that kids not old enough to see a PG movie would try and escape in the middle of the night?

After the interrogation, my mother came inside. She was not happy with us, to say the least. She couldn't figure out how this could have happened. I just kept wondering if she was going to be mad that I stole all her penny rolls. She looked at me with angry, scared eyes and asked why I would do such a thing.

I didn't know what to say at first. I had to think quickly. A simple "I don't know," wasn't going to cut it. A few seconds passed before I looked up at her with a saddened face and said, "Because I didn't think you loved me anymore." With that, her eyes softened and all was forgiven.

5

When the Saints ... Come Marching In ...

I would eventually be enrolled in a private Catholic school called St. Matthews and become shocked during that first year when I was introduced to my second-grade teacher.

She was not a tall woman by any means and definitely on the skinny side, a little too skinny. It was as if food was afraid of her and stayed away as often as possible. She had fair skin, a decent smile, and a horrible sense of fashion. She walked up to me that first day and introduced herself as Sister Virginia.

My jaw dropped! When did this happen? I grew up those first eight years or so of my life believing that my mother only had four kids, two of them being my sisters, and this woman *was not* one of them! No way; I wasn't going to believe it. I backed away from her, trying to keep as much of a visual on this imposter as humanly possible. *Just wait till I tell my mother … just watch what'll happen.*

I learned later that day that these so-called *sisters* were creatures of faith called nuns, and they meant me and my family no harm. I felt relieved and looked at my new sister of the cloth with a little less suspicion and a little more respect.

Second grade was an interesting experience for me, because things were a lot more structured than what I remembered about first grade. Things were tougher. The only thing I concerned myself with during my first-grade year in a public school was if those twin girls I saw every day at recess liked me or not. They were cuties, and I'm sure subconsciously I was banking on one of them liking me. The odds, after all, were in my favor.

But second grade … this was tougher. Private schools are smaller and more intimate. There's more attention paid to the students, which I'm sure the parents paid a great deal for the students to have. Another thing that came as a surprise to me as I was overlooking the books handed to me that first day was *Phonics*. I didn't know what it was, and I didn't like the sound of it. I had to study something called Phonics, and I was not at all happy about it!

The great thing about second grade in a private Catholic school was the friends that I made. I really only had one solid friend, but the good thing about that was that there wasn't a lot of people, so one friend in one class of thirty people was just as good as ten friends in ten classes of thirty people. My ability to win friends and influence people started at a young age, and although I didn't have strong feelings for many other people in the class, I started campaigning to become the most popular second grader in the room.

I developed a strong sense of acceptance and started to learn that young kids liked to be impressed. They liked to constantly be at a circus, and I was determined to be their full-time clown.

My strategic marketing ideas were simple: I needed to come up with ways of doing things that they never thought of doing. I needed to come up with a personality that was fresh and cool. It was the 80s, and I had plenty of mentors out there in popular culture land to pull ideas from.

One day in class during our milk time,[1] I saw that chocolate had become an option and used my supersonic hand speed to snatch up the chocolaty goodness. Looking around, I noticed that there were a bunch of eyes on me, impressed with how fast I was able to make that vitamin D grab. I now had an audience. I had no other choice but to continue with the show. I opened up one end as fast as I could, tilted that little carton to my little lips, and chugged. A few seconds later, I slammed down the empty remains and looked around the room, refusing to wipe the chocolate mustache that had formed on my upper lip.

One kid in the crowd, said, "Oooooh," and another said, "Aaaaaahhhh." I faintly heard someone in the back say, "Cool!" and I could have sworn it was Sister Virginia. Lastly, I heard a few of the girls giggle, and I nodded in acceptance as if to say, "I got it; you want it, but I'm not giving it away."

I became *that* kid. The one who could drink milk super-fast! With that newfound ability, I was the newly crowned Popular Kid in Sister Virginia's second-grade class.

Being a second-grade celebrity is not all it's cracked up to be. With it, comes a lot of responsibility. Kids are always looking up to you and requesting your expert opinion, constantly thinking that you know everything. That could be a big burden on a young person. I did the best I could, and what came out of it was my picking any girl I liked.

---

[1] Yeah, I'm serious; there was a time when they would bring in milk, and we had to drink it, followed by another time when they brought in mouthwash and we had to gargle it.

There were quite a few to choose from, but my heart told me to go with Lindsay. She was a sweet girl with a pretty face and a really nice personality. Except for a missing tooth, I was totally digging this girl, and she seemed like she cared about me for more than the fame. One day during our daily date together outside, clapping the erasers, I asked her to be my girlfriend. She said yes, and just like that, Jason Ventre, second-grade playboy was off the market. I just had to figure out a way to take this girl out on an official big-person date. She deserved no less.

I went home that night, knowing that I would need to ask for permission to go on a date with her from my parents. I didn't think that it was a big deal. Of course, I would need to borrow some money to treat Lindsay to a romantic dinner, gazing at each other over our Happy Meal boxes. Surely my mother could spare a few dollars for such a special occasion. I was feeling confident when I asked my mother for permission to go out on a date, until I saw that she looked a little taken aback by it and was unsure how to answer. She turned toward my stepfather and asked him for his opinion. *He* would eventually decide not to let me go.

I was not happy with this decision. I tried to appeal his ruling and thought that I was putting up a good argument when I told him that, "Everyone in my class was going on dates." Unfortunately, that didn't work, and the decision was made. If I remember correctly, that was the first decision my stepfather made with regards to what I could and couldn't do. There would be many to follow.

I wasn't sure how I was going to face Lindsay the next morning, but I remember dreading it. She deserved more! She deserved to be with a boy who could treat her to the finer things in life, like McDonald's Happy Meals.

When I saw her in line waiting for the bell to ring, I said hi and then put my head down. She asked what was wrong, and I felt embarrassed as tears started to form. I told her that I couldn't go on a date with her because my parents wouldn't let me. She said it was okay, and we could just keep clapping our erasers together.

She would keep to that promise, and we spent the rest of the year meeting outside at the end of the day, applauding each other until chalk smoke filled the afternoon air.

6

First Love Lost

With second grade coming to a close and my popularity level reaching heights never seen before, I was on top of the world. My grades were pretty good, all S's, I was loved and adored by all, and Lindsay and I were still clapping those erasers and staring at each other with wide-open puppy eyes. After all, we were in second grade, that's all we knew how to do. She was my first girlfriend—although that's only because I couldn't land one of the twins—and I liked her a lot, but the problem was the long time apart during the summer. I wasn't sure if we could survive that.

During our last day of school and our last eraser-clapping date, I asked Lindsay what she thought about the whole thing. Without realizing it, I was a second-grade boy requesting a trial separation! She was very sad, but said that after the summer, she wanted to go back to being my girlfriend. I was so excited, I dropped the erasers, jumped up in the air, pumped my fist, and yelled, "Yeeeeeeessssssssssssssssssssssssssss!" Hey, it was the 80s—we did that sort of thing.

When school let out, I shot out of that school like a bullet from a gun, and the wind that hit my face smelled like freedom. I had completed the second grade, and in a fashion that deserved many articles in the local tabloids. I was sure that any day the paparazzi were sure to pick up my story and hound me for the rest of my life.

When I got home after school, we were all instructed to start packing our things because our grandparents would be picking us up soon and taking us to our summertime spot on the Jersey Shore. I was super excited. Any chance to be with them was awesome. Pop (my grandfather) would spend time during the day teaching Jamie and me how to build things, while Darling (my grandmother) would cook for us and pamper us with more detail than any member of the royal family.

I started throwing clothes in a bag. I wanted to take everything, but I knew that I couldn't. It made me very sad, because my brother and I owned two My Pet Monsters, and I knew that I would miss them greatly, but I couldn't fit them in any of my bags.

I sat there staring at My Pet Monster for a while trying to explain to him the situation in hopes of earning his forgiveness. He just sat there staring back at me, not saying anything. That display of disrespect shown toward me from my furry blue friend changed the way that I looked at him, and we would never speak again.

When we finally arrived at Point Pleasant Beach, New Jersey, the smell from the ocean hit my nostrils, and I felt at peace. There was something about the shore that made me feel at home. It would take years before I figured out what that was.

Regardless, I was there, and that's all that mattered.

That summer in Jersey was great. Dani and I were hanging around the employees sitting in the booth taking in money for beach admission, and soon, my grandparents felt a need to take care of them too. One person in particular—his name was Jody—was getting pampered by Darling as much as anyone else in our family. Not only was she making *us* breakfast in the morning, but Jody was partaking in the feast as well. It was actually pretty cool to watch. Darling was running a soup kitchen full of high-quality breakfast items to the employees of the Pt. Pleasant Beach boardwalk.

Along with the amazing food, pampering, trade education, and sunny days on the beach, there were the arcades. About a half a mile down the boardwalk, it was a kid's dream. Rides and games, games and rides—it resembled the ending of the movie, *Pinocchio*, with the donkeys and cigars (minus the cigars of course).

One night after dinner, Pop asked us how much money we wanted to go down to the boardwalk with. Before anyone had a chance to offer their financial opinion, I yelled out, "Five dollars!" It was a number that seemed like a lot to me. It fact, it *was* a lot of money. I had no bills to speak of, so five dollars was five hundred percent more money than I thought I needed. Jamie got very angry with me and would scold me later for it, because he wanted to negotiate for ten dollars each.

The differences between me and my brother started to become clear from that day on. We were no longer just brothers with a four-year age difference. He was now not only older than me, but his hair was dark, while mine was light. His eyes were dark. Mine were light. He's was very tall for his age; I was a runt. He was very athletic; I wasn't as much. He led with his brain; I led with my heart.

I remember one day that summer when I was walking toward the beach, there was a group of girls that struck my eye. I didn't understand why I was drawn to them at the time. They were tall and wore different-colored paint on their eyes, and they had bumps on their chest. I normally would have thought that there was something wrong with them. They definitely weren't normal. They weren't my Lindsay.

This group of girls noticed that I was standing there staring at them, so they invited me over to hang out. Of course I did—I mean, after all, I felt that this was a great opportunity. I needed to figure out why they looked so different. When I walked up to them, I felt a little nervous at first, but they were very friendly and laughed a lot. I soon found out that they were mythical creatures call *Junior High School Girls*. I had heard of them at one point in my life, but I thought they were make-believe. Those bumps were not bumps at all, they were things called *boobies*. I didn't care what you called them; all I knew was that I liked them.

All the girls in the group were really pretty, but one girl in particular, Nelly, was the one I liked the best in the group. There was something about her that just stood out to me. She wasn't like the other girls. She wasn't as loud and chatty, but still appeared to be enjoying herself with the rest of them.

Eventually, the other girls noticed that I was looking at Nelly a little too much, and came to the conclusion that I had the *hots* for her. They started to tease me, so Nelly stood up for me and told the girls to shut up.

I was amazed at how easy it was for her to defend me, and I started to forget about Lindsay and decided that I needed to be with Nelly.

I started to imagine our life together, but before I could enjoy it, one of the girls in the group came over to me and said that Nelly had a boyfriend. I was heartbroken. The girl told me that the only way I could be with Nelly was to beat up her boyfriend. About the same time she was telling me this; a few guys were walking down the boardwalk heading toward us. One of them had a cast on his leg. The girl I was talking to pointed to the be-casted guy and said, "That's him."

Without hesitation, I sprinted over to my new enemy, determined to win the heart of my new love. When I got within attacking distance, I jumped through the air landing on his leg and attacked it like a rabid mongoose. I was relentless.

My mind after that point went blank. All I remember hearing was some high-pitched girly screams. I don't know if they were coming from the whole group of junior high school girls or from Nelly in particular, or maybe they were coming from me—had I developed my own war cry?

The story I heard later on was that my brother was the one to come running over and pull me off of that poor kid's leg before he could get the chance to beat the hell out of me.

Nelly never spoke to me again.

With many nights out on the boardwalk behind us, and my heart almost healed from the tragic loss of my future with Nelly, it was time to head back to Bristol. It was always a sad moment leaving Pop and Darling because it wasn't every day that we could see them like it had once been. They had become the grandparents that you talked to on the phone instead of being frequent visitors. That feeling was never one that my grandparents and I liked *or* approved of. I learned later in life that the time you spend away from people you love is time that you can't get back. It's time ill spent.

7

THIRD-GRADE PROBLEMS

The summer had ended and I was preparing for another grueling year in the spotlight. I knew that I would need to try and pace myself this year, because it was sure to be a long one. This was third grade. This was serious.

I wasn't as excited for this year as I had been for the first two years, because deep down inside I always had a hatred for the number 3. I just never liked it, no matter how it was written. To me, it just looked like a mean number, all pointy, as if it was directing itself at someone and accusing them of doing something wrong. Yep, I was not a big fan of the number *three*.

I also wasn't as excited to see Lindsay as I thought I would be prior to the summer starting. Granted, I was excited to be back to our eraser-clapping getaways, but I knew that I would have to come clean with her and explain what had happened that summer, even though what Nelly and I had was over.

When I waited outside in line for the bell to ring to show us to our new classroom for the year, Lindsay came up to me and we embraced in a make-believe hug. She was ecstatic to see me.

When I looked at her, I realized that I couldn't tell her what happened. I felt that the news of my infidelity could possibly ruin her for the rest of her life. She deserved more than that! I had made up my mind: I would take the secret from the brief Jersey Shore affair to the grave.

When we got to our classroom and familiarized ourselves with our new, assigned seating (a.k.a. teachers' bad-memory tool), we were handed our textbooks for the year. As a young kid, I would flip to the back of a book I was reading, because I wanted to find out how it ended. This was no different. When I turned to the last page of *Adventures in Math 3*, I noticed something a little strange. The addition signs were turned sideways and resembled an *x*. I thought for a second that the mathematicians who had made these books were wrong and somehow I'd caught the mistake. My pulse started to increase as I imagined the school giving me an award because my uncanny attention to detail had caught a mistake that would save them a lot of money from lawsuits. Think about how many parents would hire attorneys because their poor children hurt their necks turning sideways all the time just to add something up. I was going to be a hero!

With that, my hand shot up in the air. I heard someone say, "Yes?" And I turned around in my chair.

Sitting at her desk was Ms. C., our third-grade teacher. She was somewhat attractive, with big, red hair. I was relieved to see that she wasn't a nun. I kept my hand in the air.

Not knowing my name yet, she asked if she could help me with something. I said yes, and invited her over to my desk. I couldn't just blurt out loud such a delicate matter of national security. She got the hint and came over to my desk. She again asked what she could help me out with, and after I looked around to see if anyone was recording the conversation, I made her lean over and whispered in her ear, "Don't be scared, but the math books … are wrong." I showed her the back of the book where I had intercepted the error. Then I sat back in my chair and folded my arms, waiting to see how red her face would get with anger before she sprinted out the door to call the president.

She smiled at me and said, "No dear, those signs are not addition. They are called *multiplication*."

I thought to myself, *Whatchu talkin' 'bout, Willis?*

She told me that we would get to learn what multiplication was that year. And with that, she smiled again and walked away. I didn't believe her, and I started to feel what would eventually be clear to me as my First Conspiracy Theory.

There were so many things going on in my head at that time, and I felt like I needed to gather my thoughts. I took out a piece of paper, grabbed a pencil, and waited for mental clarity. I sat there for a moment, ignoring the roll call that started to take place, and by the time Ms. C. got to my name, I had come to three conclusions and wrote:

1. I don't trust Ms. C.
2. There is no such thing as this so-called "multiplication."
3. I still think the number 3 is ugly.

I felt better after I was able to get my thoughts out on paper, and went about the rest of my day.

8

The Appointment

I soon learned that third grade was hard, and I hated it. But I needed to do my best, because there were still a lot of people who looked up to me. Among those people was one kid named Ernie Migelroy. He was taller than me and about as nerdy as they come. I would have taken a chance and made friends with him, hoping that would get more people to like him, if it wasn't for the fact that he smelled like dirty laundry and old kitty litter. I just couldn't handle bad smells. He also had gigantic 80s glasses. You remember those, don't you? Well, if you have bad eyesight, somewhere in your parents' photo album, there's a picture of you in some hideous big framed '80s prescription glasses.

Anyways, I actually liked his glasses and found myself wanting a pair of them. At that time, I didn't have any problems with my eyes, but I couldn't let that get in the way of my new fashion statement. I needed to find a way to convince my mother I had bad eyes and then find a way to convince the doctor.

I went home that day excited to get Operation Big Eyes into effect. When I saw my mother, I told her that I was having a hard time seeing the board and that maybe I should have someone look at me. Being a mother, of course she said yes and scheduled the appointment for a couple of days later. I didn't think it was going to be that easy. I also needed to get briefed on what to expect, and the only one I could ask was Ernie Migelroy.

The next day at school, I pulled big Ern aside, and as if I were conducting a meeting with the head of the Scarpazzi family, I whispered to him about the appointment and explained that I was gonna need some information on how to pull this off. He told me that all I needed to do was tell the doctor that I couldn't see very well.

I said, "That's it?"

He said, "Yeah."

I said, "You sure that's it?"

He said, "Yeah."

I looked at him to see if he was telling the truth, and when I was convinced, I nodded and then showed him the backside of my hand before telling him to go take a seat before I have to give him a fresh one.

I'm just kidding I didn't threaten him.

When it was time for the appointment, I felt prepared. My inside guy had given me enough information that the situation should have been a breeze.

When my mother and I arrived at the eye doctor's office, she was given paperwork to fill out, and I sat down next to her as she was answering the questions. She seemed to know a lot about me, because she was filling out the questionnaire very quickly, and I felt close to her for some reason.

After a few moments, my name was called, so I stood up and walked toward the back, and then sat down in some small room with a bunch of weird-looking equipment. Minutes later, the doctor walked in and introduced himself as Dr. Blindside. He was a nicely dressed, friendly fellow, with a kind smile. He asked me what was going wrong, and as rehearsed, I said "Well, doctor, I just can't see very well."

He said okay and that he wanted to do some tests. *Tests?* That wasn't part of the plan. Quickly, things were starting to spiral out of control, and I needed to think.

I said, "Okay, Dr. B, but I don't think I really need to take any tests. I know that I don't see well, and I'm going to need some glasses. You have glasses here, so can't you just give me a pair, so we don't waste time?"

I thought that I had a really good recovery until Dr. Blindside blindsided me with, "I don't mind, but if we don't do any tests, I won't know the strength of the lenses you'll need."

I knew I was screwed, so in a last ditch effort, I said, "I need strong one's, doc."

He thought that was funny and with a chuckle dismissed my idea.

I said okay, but I was not happy with the situation. My inside man did *not* tell me that there was going to be a test. This was ridiculous!

The doctor settled into his chair and prepped the equipment. He told me that there were just a few tests that he would need to conduct.

The first test looked like a chart with letters on it, and I was going to have to tell him what letters were on what line. I knew I had to fail all the tests, because my vision was fine and if I passed them, I could say goodbye to my glasses. I couldn't do that. I wouldn't do that.

Dr. Blindside asked me, "What's the lowest line you can make out?"

Naturally, I said that I couldn't see any of the lines. I was instructed to read the top letter which was E. I squinted, and then I blinked. I blinked, and then I squinted. Finally, I said with confidence, "Oh yeah, I can see it now—that's an S."

Blindside stopped and looked up at me from his clipboard. He said, "Um, okay."

He asked me to try to make out the second line, which was, "I A M L Y I N G."

I said okay, and after a few more minutes of faking temporary blindness I said, "Looks like Y E S I A M."

The doctor stopped again, and there was a long pause in the room. I thought I was getting away with it so well that the guy felt bad about my blindness. Any moment now I would be out in the lobby shopping for those frames that said, "Look at me—I'm smarter than a doctor."

Blindside turned to me and said, "Well, I think I have all the information I need," and with that he walked me out to the lobby and handed me off to my mother. She asked me how everything went, and Dr. B asked her if he could speak with her in private. She said yes, and they walked away.

Naturally, I start walking around the lobby trying on various types of frames. I wasn't sure if I wanted to go with the all-favorable silver frames or stick with the gold. Jamie wore glasses and had tortoise-colored frames, and I was *not* all about those. I couldn't quite make up my mind which ones looked the best on me, and I was about to temporarily give up on my search, when I spotted the perfect pair. They were silver and round, and when I tried them on and looked in the mirror, I became even more attractive. If I do say so myself. I looked established, well educated. I looked like an attorney!

I started to think about myself appearing in court to give my closing statement of the prosecution to send the worst criminal in history straight to jail for the rest of his life. I stood and then walked over to the jurors. With a fire in my heart and conviction in my throat, I delivered that statement with everything I had, begging for a conviction! When I was done, I looked over at them. The women were looking down at their watches, and the men were sleeping. I thought to myself, *Hmm...this isn't working.*

I walked over to my table, opened my eyeglass case, and put on my new frames. Then, as if I were in a Vidal Sassoon commercial, I whipped my head around toward them, my long, soft hair flying behind me in slow motion. I could see the women starting to sweat, and the men starting to clap. There would be no deliberation. The foreman stood up, trying to fan herself with her hand, and yelled, "Guilty!" The audience started yelling and cheering. I was *the man.*

Then the judge stood up and as he hammered his gavel down ... I blinked, and the next thing I knew, my mother was walking very fast toward me, and as she passed me she said, "Let's go!"

I didn't know what was happening. All I knew was that I wasn't in the courtroom anymore, I was no longer successful, I wasn't established, and I wasn't getting glasses.

I don't know what Blindside told her, but since I wasn't getting glasses, I'm sure it was along the lines of, "Um, yeah, your son is full of shit." Damn doctors and their damn tests! Who do they think they are taking away a kid's dream? To this day, every time I pass an eye doctor's office, my blood pressure rises and I have an uncontrollable urge to growl.

9

BREAKING UP IS HARD TO DO

When I got back to school that next day, I was met by all my cronies and their excitement to see me in my new glasses. Big Ern had opened his big mouth and told *everyone* that I had the appointment. I was so pissed off at him as it was. I wanted to get back at him for his shitty advice. I wasn't going to go off and get in a fight with the poor kid, but I had to teach him a lesson. With the group surrounding me growing larger, asking to see my glasses, I held up my hand and said, "You guys want to see my glasses? Why would I have those?"

One girl said, "Well, Ernie told us you were getting them."

I replied with, "I can't get glasses, those are for nerds."

With that, the group laughed, Ernie cried, and I felt better about myself.

Side note to Big Ern: Sorry buddy. I didn't mean to make you cry.

***

At the end of the day, Lindsay and I were at our normal spot, when she timidly brought up the fact that we hadn't even kissed yet. I hadn't even thought of that! I started to get nervous about it. She made it seem like it was bothering her, so I told her that we would kiss tomorrow.

I was nervous about this whole first kiss thing. I mean, I understood the gist of it, but wouldn't our noses prevent us from getting in there? I guess we could always turn our heads, but which way do we turn them? Was I supposed to go right as she goes left or the other way around? The anxiety from all these unanswered questions started to make me very scared of the whole process. I couldn't just go home and ask for the advice of my big brother, because he was too busy playing video games without me. Kellie would just laugh at me, and Dani would probably say, "Who cares? Wanna go outside and throw the football around?" I was running out of people I could ask to help me figure this whole thing out. I thought of asking my parents, but they weren't okay with the idea of me hanging out with this girl at Mickey D's, let alone getting it on in school.

I couldn't sleep that night. I felt alone. This was a big moment in my life. How many *first*, first kisses do you get in life? I felt like that one kid on the baseball team with no one rooting for him in the stands. I thought that maybe a bowl of Cheerios would get my mind off things. After all, it has the word *cheery* in it; couldn't do any harm, right?

I was exhausted by the time I got to school, and I'm sure my face showed it. Normally I would have probably fallen asleep right there at my desk, if it had not been for the head principal woman walking in the door and introducing a new student to the room. Her name was Nicole. She had curling-iron-curled hair and piercing blue eyes, very similar to my own. I had a hard time keeping my eyes off of her. She looked right at me and smiled as if to say, "Hey, if you want, I'll share my Oreo's with you."

I did a double take and immediately turned around to see if anyone else noticed the look that girl just gave me. Instead of getting my answer, all I got when I turned around was a look from Lindsay that said, "You ain't sharin' shit" (assuming third-grade girls think like a thirty-year-old black woman.) Then she smiled and reminded me about our little lip appointment outside. For a brief moment, I had forgotten about kissing one girl because I was checking out a different one!

I didn't eat anything for lunch that day because my stomach was in knots, and I spaced out the rest of the day, because I couldn't get my mind off of kissing Nicole ... uh ... I mean Lindsay. See what I mean?

When the end of the day arrived, I grabbed the erasers and walked with Lindsay outside. She was acting very shy. I felt like I was going to throw up my Cheerios. I needed to say something to her. If I wasn't going to make my move, I at least needed to be honest and tell her that I really liked her and was totally excited about kissing her but had been nervous since yesterday and didn't have anyone to talk to about it.... Minutes passed and the erasers were running out of chalk. I decided to count down from five and then tell her what I was thinking. Five, four, three, two, one—I opened my mouth and said, "Lindsay, I'm sorry, but I can't be your boyfriend anymore." She didn't have time to ask why. I threw the erasers, ran into the building, past the classroom, into the bathroom, and locked myself in a stall.

When I heard the bell ring dismissing the kids for the day, I sprinted out of the bathroom and down the hall. I passed my classroom, leaving my books behind, and didn't stop running until I got home.

I had no idea how I was going to live this one down. I was the cool kid ... who was afraid of some kisses. What kind of example was I setting for my people?

The next day at school I ignored everyone, and Lindsay ignored me. I felt bad for telling her like that, but what else was I supposed to say? When it was our time to take care of the erasers, we stood there in silence until I said, "I'm sorry, but my parents said that I can't have a girlfriend anymore."

She said okay, and with that out of the way, I was now free to go after Nicole.

The rest of third grade wasn't very eventful. I became Nicole's boyfriend and pissed off Lindsay. Called it off with Nicole, because I felt bad about Lindsay, and then Lindsay dumped me for some reason that was never made clear. The shelf life of a relationship in third grade was not very high, and I think it had to do with the broad array of available snack foods on the market. Think about it: if Lindsay has some Oreo's on Monday, I'd wanna be with her, but if Nicole came in on Tuesday with some Chips-Ahoys, bye-bye Lindsay. Hell, if Blanche, the token fat girl ever came in with some fruit roll ups, then I guess I would have gone chubby chasing. Love has no loyalty. It does have a remarkable sense of taste and an incredible sense of humor.

Other than that, I managed to pass third grade despite my refusal to complete any assignments that had anything to do with this so called, "Multiplication." I had more important things to worry about. The summer was upon me, and that meant another summer with Pop and Darling. What more could a kid want?

Jersey was the same that summer as the summers prior to it. It was always very consistent. We were all spoiled, and I'm not going to say that we didn't love it, because we did. Darling *always* did everything she could to make us happy, and Pop was right there behind her doing the same. The only thing that was really missing was Nelly. I looked for her that summer, but didn't find her.

IO

Fourth-Grade Issues

The summer had ended, and I was heading off to this thing called *fourth grade*. I had somehow passed the third grade, and I was starting to see a pattern. If you passed a grade with a number like 3, then 4 was next. When I realized this, I patted myself on the back, because I was clearly learning, and I would soon be the next Einstein.

Unfortunately, fourth grade proved to be difficult right off the bat. For starters, it seemed to me that fewer and fewer kids were talking to me, and I somehow found myself outside of the cool group. I didn't know what the hell was going on! I know that at one point the year before, this girl by the name of Emily Plant saw me picking my nose. I used to make fun of her last name, so I started to wonder if she told everyone to get back at me. I would bet that's how I lost my following.

I was starting to feel like I hated St. Matthews. I wanted to get as far away from there as I could. I stood there on the blacktop waiting for the first bell to ring, when my buddy, Matty B., walked over and said hello. Then more kids came over, and once again, I was on top of the world. I was the *man!*

When we got into our new fourth-grade classroom, we were introduced to our teacher. Her name was Ms. Heartastone. She was a short woman with short, dirty-blonde hair and a desire to teach. A little too much desire, if you ask me. She was like a German soldier with a teacher's certificate. This woman scared the shit out of me! The only thing she was missing was an accent and a swastika. I admired her passion, but at the same time, not really.

I went through the normal ritual of laying all my books out on my desk and then reading the back of them. Of course, in the math book, the damn *x*'s were present. I was not happy about that. I guess I just assumed that over the summer they would leave, because I had made it very clear how much I didn't like them. I thought it to be common sense. Shoot, I don't like to stay in an area where I'm not liked; do you?

But nope, they were there, and I just sighed thinking that I was going to have another year of arguing with their validity.

Looking around the room, I started to once again familiarize myself with the faces I remembered, receiving smiles as I went from one to the next—until I came to Nicole's. She had a scowl on her face. Of course, she had started a Jason Ventre hate group with Lindsay, so after getting the stink eye from Nicole, Lindsay's stink eyes were right behind. I'm sure that if you were to fast-forward ten years or so, you'd see both of those girls marching in one of those pride parades.

When I was almost finished scanning the room with my eyes, I stopped at a very unfamiliar face. Our classroom was a very tight-knit family—with me as the head of the group of course. I was confused about who this kid thought he was, just coming in the room, sitting down, and thinking that he could breathe my educational air. I grew angry with him, but felt that even though he was trying to be one of us, he wasn't, and I needed to find out everything about him that I could.

I got up and went over to Big Ern's desk and told him that I was giving him a chance to redeem himself. I said that I needed as much information as I could get on this intruder. He nodded, accepting the mission with his big, dumb glasses that I wanted so badly. I went back to my seat and sat down, feeling good that there were so many people I could call on for a favor.

A few minutes later, Ms. Heartastone walked to the front of the room, her heels hammering the ground in a cadence that could make any private shake in his boots. When she got there, she did an about-face, and when her head whipped around, it stopped at me. What the hell was she looking at? I didn't know why, but it was making me nervous. I wasn't sure whether I should get up and fight this woman or get down and do some pushups. I decided to do nothing, but instead just sat there and stared back at her, occasionally crossing my eyes to see if I could break her concentration. I was unsuccessful.

When she decided to break the silence, she opened with, "Good Morning. As you now know, my name is Ms. Gertrude Heartastone. I will be your fourth-grade teacher." She started pacing the room, and I started sweating a little. I don't think she knew that the war was over. She then stopped and came over to my desk and stood there. She opened her mouth again, and the words flowed out just as hard as the last time as she said, "Most of you have been together for quite some time and know each other very well. A strong team is a great team, but sometimes, new teammates can make the team even stronger. So, the next time you want to know why someone is in your class, remember that this is *not* your class. This is *my* class. This is *our* team, and no one is above the team."

With that, she paused for another few seconds in front of me and heel-hammered back to her desk. I couldn't believe it! Big Ern dimed me out! When I asked for his help, he must have gone over to Sgt. Slaughter and told her what I told him! This would require some more payback.

The new kid's name was Timmy Tilapovich. He was about my height, but a little tanner. That was the first thing I didn't like about him. Judging by his last name, he was *not* Italian and had no right to try to unintentionally *out-tan* me. I started to feel angry and wondered if I was being stupid. Was a tan on a new face enough to make me that angry? After many minutes of staring at this guy, I decided that it wasn't enough. I turned and faced the front of the room. I remember feeling my pulse start to slow. I smiled to myself as I thought of how stupid it was to let a better tan affect me.

A few minutes later, the door opened, and our milk was wheeled in. It was one of my favorite times of the day. I knew that it was my time to shine again, like it had been every day for the last couple of years. Everyone got up and walked over to collect their little carton of dairy delight, and I waited at the back of the line with Timmy in front of me. I knew that when I got up to the milk cart, there would be chocolate milk waiting for me. As the line got shorter and shorter, and I got closer and closer, I noticed that there were a few white milks left, but only one chocolate. I didn't think that was too out of the ordinary. It was evident that the kids in the class saved the last one for me, because they were very eager to see the show. When Timmy got up to the cart, I expected him to just grab a white milk and take his seat like the rest of the common folk in the classroom, but he didn't. That little shit took the last chocolate milk, and I could have sworn that when he turned around and passed me, he gave me a little smirk!

I stood there shocked! I stared at that milk tray for many seconds as if I was expecting a chocolate milk to just all of a sudden show up and say, "Hey, I'm sorry I was late. You can drink me now." Nope, no chocolate milk. We were completely out. I knew that my patience was starting to wear very thin for Tilapovich. He was not only a tan Russian kid, but now he was drinking my chocolate milk. This had to stop!

I picked up the tiny carton of boring ol' white milk and walked back to my seat. At first, a few of the kids saw me with the white milk and, after a few whispers, flew across the room; it seemed everyone was looking over at me. I wasn't sure if they were excited to see the daily milk chugging show, or they were as shocked as I was to see me with a container of white milk in my hands. Either way, they were looking, and it was time for the show to begin.

Turning toward Tilapovich, I aggressively opened the milk, held it in the air, chugged it, and then slammed down the empty carton.

I felt good about myself. I also felt that I probably set a new record. I drank that milk faster than I remember ever drinking it before. A couple people in the audience clapped, and immediately I heard Heartastone yell for them to stop clapping, but I didn't care. Little Timmy was sent a letter, and in it was a note that said, "Get out of my house."

My smile couldn't possibly get any bigger than it was at that moment, until the darnedest thing happened. Lil' ol' Tim-Tim grabbed the carton of chocolate milk that was *supposed* to be mine, ripped open the top, and chugged it down faster than I had! He topped off the show by slamming his carton down faster than I'd slammed mine down. I heard some kid yell "OOOOH!," some other kid yell, "AHHHHH!"; and if I heard correctly, I think Heartastone might have clapped.

My face got red, and my hands started to shake! I needed to do something to retaliate. He was now staring at me. I couldn't have this happen. I couldn't lose control of my crew. I stared back at that little tan, cocky, fast-milk-drinking kid and said the only thing that I could in a moment of crisis such as that: "Oh yeah? Well, I bet you can't run faster than me." Naturally, all eyes were on us and as soon as I said that, all you could hear in the class were whispers. I had slapped him in the face with the imaginary white glove. There was no way he was going to accept my challenge, but even if he did, he wasn't going to win. There was no way. I was too fast for him. The weight from his tan alone would hold him back.

I started to look around the room with confidence after calling this kid out, and smiled at everyone in hopes of reassuring them that I was still their leader and that everything was going to be okay. When I turned back toward my new enemy, he uttered the words that to this day get my heart racing: "We'll see about that."

The room went silent. My face went blank. And I could start to feel a fire building in the pit of my stomach. We looked at each other for what seemed like a few days, and neither one of us wanted to break the stare. To show him that I meant business, I grabbed my empty white-milk carton in both hands, held it up in the air, and squeezed it until it was a tiny, empty white-milk carton. I smiled as I slammed it down on the desk. I knew he was mine. I owned this kid. But my smile was short-lived when I saw him pick up his empty chocolate-milk carton and squeezed it with ONE hand! I swallowed hard and knew that this might end badly for me.

The rest of the morning went by as it normally would on the first day of school. We didn't learn much. Most of the focus was on getting situated and going over each subject that we were going to learn, including a serious emphasis on *History*. I didn't know why: it already happened; it can't change; so why did we have to learn it?

Those questions, however, at that time, didn't mean all that much to me, because I had the great race to think about. My reputation and everything I had worked so hard for was on the line. I couldn't just let someone with a tan I wanted and milk-drinking abilities that I envied take that away from me! I had to get my head right. I needed to mentally prepare for this great victory. I was the fastest kid on that blacktop. That was a fact.

When the bell rang for recess, everyone stampeded out the back door in anticipation for what was going to happen. I walked out pumped up and ready to show the world that I was the best. When we lined up to start the race, I looked over at him and slid my thumb across my neck showing the universal sign for, "I'm going to kill you," and with that, we both took off. Timmy shot off that line like a fat kid chasing a speeding ice-cream truck! All I saw was a blur and what looked like smoke coming out from under his shoes. I don't even remember finishing the race. I was in a state of shock. This kid was a freakin' robot. It just wasn't fair. I didn't understand how it could happen. How could someone be *that* fast? It would take me eight years before I would come to the conclusion that T-Rod was not a robot, but just an average, normal, run-of-the-mill fourth grader … on steroids.

II

MUTINY

From that point on, I saw a dramatic shift in power from the Jason Ventre regime to Mr. T's. I was really sad about it. I had worked so hard to be the kid that all the other kids could look up to. I'm sure the damage I probably caused to my esophagus by drinking all those milks like that was evidence enough of the sacrifices I had made for these ungrateful kids. What did Timmy have that I didn't have? Sure, he had a better tan and could drink milk and run faster than me, but *that* was it! There was so much more that I could offer than those three amazing qualities. What about my ability to clean erasers, huh? Aside from Lindsay, no one else in that school had more ability and experience in banging those things. Could he do that? I felt myself starting to pull away from everyone. I hated fourth grade. I hated this school. I hated my teacher. I hated all of the mutinous traders I once cared for, and after finding out that Timmy was an expert on something referred to as the Multiplication Tables, I hated him even more!

With the start of fourth grade not going as well as I had hoped, I remember feeling sad, and it was a feeling that didn't go away all year. I stayed to myself for most of that year, and my grades suffered because of it. I had gone from the life of the group to feeling like the lice-infested kid that no one wants to play with. I didn't realize it at the time, but I was legitimately depressed, and it was something I had no control over. I remember feeling that the whole world was against me, and I had no one to talk to.

Luckily enough, martial arts was popular back then, and I fell in love with it. Bruce Lee was my favorite hero, and up until watching him on film, I felt that I didn't have anyone else to turn to. I didn't have anyone to talk to. He would fill that void. I watched as many of his films as I could. I felt close to him. At one point, I started praying to him, using a telephone pole as my church. Of course by that point, my mother, stepfather, and siblings thought that I was a lunatic and would, to this day, make fun of me for believing that Bruce Lee was stuck in a telephone pole. I didn't care, though. Every kid plays make-believe, but this kid had a reason to do it. I felt at a young age that I was the outcast of the family. I felt that no one really understood me, so if I had to talk to telephone poles and they didn't like it, who gives a shit? There is no such thing as bad publicity, and I was finally getting attention from them, albeit not the *exact* kind that I was looking for.

When the attention started to run out, I made the announcement that I wanted to be a DJ. That career dream was believed and supported about as much as the time I announced I wanted to be a doctor. That is, not much.

Getting myself up in the morning for school was getting harder and harder by the day. I didn't want to be there, but there was some stupid law about having to stay in fourth grade. I didn't like the rule, but I didn't have a choice. One morning in particular, I really didn't want to go, because there was going to be a history test. I hated tests. I didn't understand the point of them. I was happy to admit that I didn't know any of the answers to the questions that were going to be on it, so why did I have to prove that in writing? It's like schools are purposely trying to make children feel more inferior than they already feel, after living a life full of rocky relationships and telephone-pole praying. Nonetheless, I did something that day that I never normally did. I studied.

The next morning, I sat in that classroom and was eventually handed the history test. I grabbed my number two pencil and read over the questions. Oddly enough, there were quite a few that I somehow knew the answer to, and I quickly circled those answers. This test had been "numerous-choice"—I refused to say "*multiple*-choice"—and I liked it because I had a chance of guessing right. My heart always dropped when I'd get handed a test with blank lines next to the questions, so numerous-choice was good for me.

The rest of the questions, I didn't really know; so I circled what I thought was the answer that made the most sense. I turned in the test and sat back, knowing that I'd done just as well as I always did, which wasn't good at all.

The next day when I walked into class in the morning, I was met by Ms. Heartastone and the principal. They didn't have welcoming smiles on their faces, and I knew something wasn't right. They sat me down and, with concern, showed me the results of the history test. I had somehow managed to score 100 percent! I couldn't believe it! I was probably more shocked than they were. At the same time, I didn't understand why they weren't happy about it. They just stood there, like they had just found out I was the one who had stolen their car and they wanted answers as to why I had done it.

I nervously smiled at them and waited anxiously for one of them to speak. Ms. Heartastone was the first to do so by saying, "Jason, we're concerned about the results from this test."

I said, "Okay, why is that? It looks like I did great." I couldn't understand why they were so angry.

The principal said, "Jason, Ms. Heartastone has been telling me that you've had a hard time in school this year, especially to do with math and history, so we find it troubling that you were able to score 100 percent on this test."

I immediately caught their hinting, and I started to feel offended by the accusation. Who the fuck were these bitches? They were supposed to be called *teachers*, not *accusers*! I started to get angry and refused to answer any more questions. They were going to have to take it up with my mother, and they sure did.

I couldn't tell you what happened when they called my mother that day, but what I can tell you, is that I remember not being punished for anything. That would lead me to believe that my parents were in my corner. I wish I could remember, because if I knew for sure that they were, I probably would feel a little closer to them.

I do, however, remember one story in particular where my mother stood up for me. During that same year, after all I'd been through, I had become bitter and jaded. I didn't want to be friends with *anyone* and ignored as many people as I could. At that school, whenever there was a birthday, the class did what any class should do, they sang "Happy Birthday" to the birthday student.

Well, this particular day had left me feeling that they didn't deserve to hear the vocal abilities that I possessed. Heartastone didn't like that, and after the song was over, she started to yell at me about not singing. I didn't care what she had to say, and told her that I was not going to sing "Happy Birthday," no matter what. Of course, as horrible teachers do, she made a phone call home to my mother. When my mom heard what I was getting yelled at for, she got mad and started yelling at the teacher. I heard her say, "If my son doesn't want to sing "Happy Birthday," then he isn't going to sing "Happy Birthday!" and with that, she hung up the phone.

I felt close to her that day, and whether I got all the words she yelled at Ms. Heartastone correct or not, she stuck up for me, and I'll never forget that. My mother showed me that day that there was some sort of love for me. It was great!

❖❖❖

Fourth grade was coming to a close and my grades hadn't improved. One day, my mother came over to me and said that the school had suggested that I repeat the fourth grade. I was NOT at all happy about this! How was I supposed to be expected to go through that shit again? Luckily enough, we had all received word that Heartastone was *not* going to be teaching again the following year, so that made me happy, but unfortunately for me, the librarian, Mrs. Spellbinder would be taking her place.

Mrs. S. was a tall woman with an oddly shaped body that would only make sense if it belonged to a librarian. She was kind of pear-shaped, but an old and wrinkly pear, with an annoying voice that gave me chills every time I heard it. I told my mother that I couldn't do it. I couldn't go through a whole year of that woman's voice. On top of that, I had checked out the library book *The Polar Express* and somehow misplaced it. Once a week for almost a whole year, I'd spent dodging this woman, and I was doing a great job, but I wouldn't be able to do it every day in the same classroom.

I explained to my mother that I wasn't willing to repeat the fourth grade. She told me that it was just a suggestion, and the school couldn't force me to do it. She said that inevitably, it would be up to me. She also told me that she and my stepfather had purchased a house in Torrington, Connecticut, and we would be moving after the school year ended; so I wouldn't have to repeat the fourth grade with that teacher in that school anyway. I wasn't surprised at the idea of moving again, and it didn't faze me, but the thought of not having to be at St. Matthews was kind of exciting to me. I still wasn't convinced about repeating the same grade though.

My mother said okay, and as she was walking away, she said, "Oh, by the way, your father repeated fourth grade, and he turned out to be fine." With that, I agreed, and we spent the remainder of the year packing for the big move to a town called Torrington, Connecticut.

I didn't have to really worry about my grades for the rest of the year, because I was going to have to do it all over again anyway, so what was the worst thing they could do to me?

As far as I was concerned, I was done with Bristol; I was done with St. Matthews; I was done with the traitors in that class, and most importantly, I was done with Ms. Heartastone.

PART 2

12

TORRINGTON

The house we were moving to in Torrington was a big upgrade compared to what we had in Bristol. It was a four-bedroom home, and it was a lot larger. When you first walked in the front door, you were met with a very open two-story foyer, grounded by shiny hardwood floors throughout the large, open-concept dining and family room. My mother had a thing for very open and airy entrances. It was a simple house with plenty of room for the kids. The basement was probably the coolest part of the house, because it was like a kid's imagination playground. You could do anything and be anyone you wanted with that much space.

The neighborhood that we moved into was the epitome of suburban America. Everyone's grass was green and neatly manicured. The fences were freshly painted, and the yards were small! Our neighbors all had kids who were around the ages of my siblings and me, so there was always someone to hang out with.

All the neighbors were friendly except for one family. They were the Schmelsons, and they were weird! The father, Billy Schmelson, was a bit of a dick. He never really had anything good to say. He would just wash his Honda Civic hatchback every weekend with his head down, as if he was too afraid to make eye contact with anyone. He was a very peculiar man. He and his wife had two kids. Their names were Duddley and Meribeth. Duddley and Meribeth Schmelson. They were just as odd as their father. Duddley liked to pull out his *little* Duddley and show the world that he could make it look like an accordion. Meribeth was just socially awkward. She attended a private school, and I could picture her being the type of girl who steals other girls' undies and collects them in a box under her bed. Yeah, she was THAT weird.

Another really cool part about this neighborhood was the fact that the builders were still building, and it would stay that way for years to come. So they left gigantic mountain-sized piles of dirt and stuff for us to play on. I knew that I liked this neighborhood the second I laid eyes on it.

13

GRADE 4.2

The summer flew by quicker than any summer I could remember. We accomplished a lot, what with moving and going to Jersey and getting situated for school. It was a lot of work, and before I knew it, the summer was over, and it was time to start my second year in fourth grade for the first time.

Having to repeat the fourth grade didn't bother me as much as it did at first. I had finally come to terms with it, and I would make the most out of it. I also figured that I had a year of experience on these first-time fourth graders, and maybe with that superior knowledge, I could start another Jason Ventre following. Of course, I would need a slammin' outfit for the first day of school if I was to accomplish this. I no longer had to wear a uniform. I needed to quickly find out what was cool nowadays.

After watching many MTV videos, I knew what I had to wear! They were called Skids, and they were parachute-like pants with crazy neon colors and the Skid patch on the back. You HAD to have that patch on the back or you just weren't cool. As luck be a lady, my mother decided to buy me the ones that *looked* just like the real Skids, but were in fact missing that patch. I normally would have been very upset with my mother's minute inattention to detail, but she had a lot of kids to clothe, and I was excited for my new school, so I didn't let it bother me that much. I was now a public school kid. I was hardcore. I started to feel unstoppable.

The transition was a big one for me, but I didn't care. The mere size difference in the school itself was something to keep you in a state of shock, let alone the cafeteria and blacktop. There was much more than one fourth-grade class. This school had everything.

When it was time for the students to report to their class, I happily got in line and was guided into the classroom where I would spend the rest of my fourth-grade year, hopefully graduating this time.

I took my seat, and a few minutes later, a ridiculously tall gentleman by the name of Mr. Smitty Lurchel walked in and introduced himself as our fourth-grade teacher. I swallowed the wrong way and started to cough out loud—in chat room lingo, COL. I couldn't believe what I just heard! He was going to be our teacher for the WHOLE year, and HE wasn't a SHE! I thought that *all* teachers were supposed to be girls. Who was this poser? There was no way he was a teacher. Teachers didn't resemble Abraham Lincoln. I gave Mr. Lurchel the stinky retinas, and I felt a suspicious feeling in the pit of my stomach. I would need to keep *both* eyes on this guy.

We were all eventually handed our books for the year, and like I always did, I flipped right to the back. I didn't want to waste time. I needed to know how this whole thing was going to end. Sitting next to me was a boy by the name of Jesse, and he seemed like a nice kid right off the bat. Now I don't know what came over me, but without even thinking, I looked at Jesse and said, "This year is going to be totally easy! These books are the same ones that I used last year at my old school."

Of course they weren't. I blatantly lied, and I didn't understand why. Jesse said, "Cool," and went back to looking through the books that I was supposedly an expert in. I didn't realize why I felt a need for acceptance by lying like that, but I couldn't help it. Something in me had changed. I don't know what it was, but now I was lying, and there was no lying about that.

To say it nicely, Mr. Lurchel was an interesting fellow. His height alone made him look awkward. Combine that with his wrinkly skin, odd preference in facial hair, and the thousand-yard stare that just said, "Hi, I'm creepy and will probably give you nightmares." He was also very old-school with his ways of disciplining the kids in my class when they were doing something wrong. Instead of calling our parents, he would make us write over and over again what we "wouldn't" do the next time. For example, one time I had to write, "I will not put a frog in the pencil sharpener again; I will not put a frog in the pencil sharpener again, etc. etc....." I mean, you do something *one* time, and people look down on you forever about it.

One day during class, I was quite bored with whatever it was we were learning, so I decided to start completing those written punishments before I even committed them. It was my own little insurance policy. Instead of doing school work, which I was not a big fan of, I decided to proactively and preemptively pay for any punishments I might end up committing. This plan was genius! Mr. Lurchel was so obvious about how he would have us word our punishment assignments that I could take time out of the school day to write up whatever it was I was probably going to do in the future. Unfortunately, the other kids in the classroom saw what I was doing and wanted in on it. I told them that they couldn't, because I came up with the idea first, and for some strange reason they bought that and asked if I could make some for them. Naturally, I said yes, and thus, opened the doors to my first business. I was an insurance salesman specializing in Written Punishment Trafficking.

Business was good, and I wasn't complaining. At first, I didn't require money for my services, but what I *did* require was neatly and accurately completed homework assignments. I enjoyed going home at the end of the day and writing those prepunishment policies over and over again, instead of having to deal with the frustration of not knowing something I should know, considering this was my second attempt at this whole fourth-grade thing.

A few weeks later, I had sold enough punishment assignments to last me the rest of the year without having to do any more homework. I felt a need at that point to try to expand my operation and would eventually start selling my written services for test answers. On *numerous*-choice tests, for example, if I didn't know the answer to a question, I would hold out a number of fingers to go with the numbered question, and if the kids to my sides knew the answer, they would hold out a certain number of fingers to go with the answer. Example:

1 finger = A

2 fingers = B

Etc., etc. ...

If the kid behind me knew the answer, he would tap the leg of my chair the number of fingers he would have held up had he been sitting next to me.

This went on for another couple of weeks or so until I started to fail too many tests. Apparently, the kids I was selling my services to were about as bad at taking tests as I was. I realized it was time to change my fee from test answers to money. During my first money exchange, I got caught by Lurchel. He demanded that I hand in all of my fraudulent work or ... he would make a phone call home.

I couldn't believe it! Lurchel was NEVER this demanding. He gave me no choice. I had to do what I had to do. The next day I handed Lurchel all of my hard work, and he told the class that whatever arrangements were made to acquire these documents was now canceled. The shit had hit the fan, and I was no longer in business. Lurchel swooped in like a gigantic Wal-Mart and put my little business out of business. I was no longer a trafficker of finely written punishment insurance.

14

Short Lived

With no money, homework assignments, or test answers coming in, I was forced to start to learn this *school* stuff all by myself. Hey, what's a kid to do?

Shortly after the whole "trafficking" incident, Lurchel moved our seats around to shake things up a little bit more. My new neighbor was a really short kid named Gordon Stumpit. He was a dorky little guy with huge glasses and a couple of moles. I also remember him very clearly because of the way he held his pencil. Don't ask me to describe it, because the best authors out there wouldn't be able to do it. All I can tell you is that he used too many fingers, and I didn't like it. He also had one of those really nerdy voices. Kind of like a cross between Steve Erkel and a dying cat. I didn't hold that against him though, because he was really smart and I knew he would be able to help me out with my studies.

After watching how Gordon conducted himself during the day, I started to wonder if I could be as smart as he was just by mimicking what he did. So I tried it. I changed my voice a little. I even hunched my back over and started to walk a little dorkier. A couple of days later, I didn't feel smarter and my next graded homework assignment was even lower than it usually was. Things were looking bad for me—I didn't want to have to go through the fourth grade for a third time. I was getting desperate. I needed to figure out the easiest way to get through this cursed grade. I knew that if I could just get to the fifth grade, everything would be okay.

I started to imagine myself being Mr. Lurchel, but instead of teaching the class, I was still in it. I couldn't let this happen. I needed to come up with a plan to prevent this educational apocalypse. I closed my eyes and concentrated very hard. Seconds later, the answer jumped out at me like a hungry, hungry hippo! I needed to get back to my cheating ways. That was it!

First, I tried blatantly cheating off of Stumpit's paper, but after allowing me to do that a few times, he said he couldn't do it anymore. Then, I tried to cheat off his paper without him knowing, and he caught me. He wasn't happy. I didn't know what his problem was. He was being really selfish, and I started to not like him as much.

To make Gordon a little jealous over our diminishing relationship, I went out and found some new friends. These guys had "cool" stamped right on them. No, seriously, they used to write "cool" all over their arms. They also taught me how to swear, and I was doing it as often as I could.

The F word was no longer just the word that you would occasionally use to show anger, oh no! I began to use it every chance I got ... when I found myself away from my parents. It got to the point that I was using it too much, and the cool kids pulled me aside and told me to calm down all the swearing. I was kind of surprised because it was *those* guys that taught me how to do it! They told me that they were concerned, because if I was swearing that much away from my parents, then chances were, I would slip one day and swear around my parents. They said that maybe I should start abbreviating the swear words instead, because that's not bad—I couldn't get in trouble by doing that. I understood what they were saying and thanked them for the advice.

The very next day at school we had a pop quiz, and I was pissed! No one said *anything* about this to us. Lurchel could have at least told ME about it! The nerve of that guy! I had been *lurcheled* and there was nothing anyone could do about it. Halfway through the allotted test time, I realized that I didn't know *any* of the answers, and I decided to let my eyes wander over to Stumpit's paper. He caught me trying to cheat and had had enough of it. Immediately, his hand shot up in the air like a bullet, and he said, "That's it, I'm telling on you."

I knew I was screwed so punched him in the arm and yelled, "Eff you, you effin' A-hole." Now of course, that type of vulgarity caught Lurchel's attention, and he came flying over like a starved vampire. Lurchel got right in between us and was defensively preparing himself to break up a fight. Stumpit sat there crying and rubbing his arm. The good news was that the blow from the solidly placed arm punch jammed Stumpit's memory, and he forget to tell Lurchel that I was cheating. The bad news was that Lurchel felt that he needed to call home and tell my parents that I was blatantly screaming choice words at poor defenseless students during a test.

I had mixed feelings about the phone call, because on one hand, the cool kids said I couldn't get in trouble for saying those abbreviations, because it wasn't really swearing. On the other hand, Lurchel never called his other students' parents, so he apparently didn't share the opinions of my cool friends. What's that expression? "Keep your friends close, but keep the idiots that teach you how to swear far away?"

When I got home after school, my parents were waiting for me. My stepfather now had a few years of parenting experience and took the lead role in questioning me about the sudden vulgar outburst in school. He wanted to know why I was swearing like that. Naturally I denied everything. What nine-year-old kid wouldn't? He laid out the evidence of the phone call on the metaphorical table in front of me and waited for my response. I continued to deny it. He continued to show it. I eventually decided to compromise and tell him that I didn't *really* swear. He asked me what I *really* said. So I told him that I was being picked on by this bully at school and I called him an "Effin' A-hole." Immediately my stepfathers face got red. He asked me why I lied to him. I was kind of surprised at his newest accusation toward me. I said, "I didn't lie to you. I told you I didn't swear because saying 'Effin' A-hole' is not a swear."

He felt differently about that, and now he was mad at me for swearing AND lying to him. I don't remember what my sentence was for that crime, but I'm sure it wasn't a good one. Gordon Stumpit and I would never speak again.

15

SENTENCING

Punishments in our house were always lame. If we didn't get a spanking or yelled at or grounded, we would have things taken away from us. Growing up, we didn't have much for our parents to take away. We never had a TV in our rooms. We didn't have a phone in our rooms. No one had cell phones back then or iPods. Aside from a Nintendo, which I never owned, we didn't grow up with any of the shit that kids grow up with nowadays. That being said, the only things that my parents could take away were things that they considered to be *Privileges*. They felt that the bedtime you were given was a *privilege*. They felt that the amount of time you could play outside after school was a *privilege*. They also felt that dating was a privilege. I absolutely hated that punishment.

I was always getting into trouble because I always wanted to stand out from the crowd. Different was okay with me. I never wanted to blend in with the crowd. I had opinions. I had views. I had an uncontrollable desire to be someone that other people wanted to be. I guess when you're younger and you want to stand out, it takes too much time to do it the hard way by excelling in something, so you tend to lean toward doing something that could be wrong to build that popularity faster. I was that kid, but I didn't care. I fed off that admiration, no matter the cost to earn it.

My parents, on the other hand, seemed to want to sabotage my rise in power. They were always taking away the things that I needed to become more popular. For example, *Beverly Hills 90210* was a really popular TV show, especially with the girls, and my bedtime would allow for me to watch it. This was a really good thing, because the information I gained by watching the show gave me enough conversational material to talk to just about any girl in my grade. But as our family punishments would go, if I did something wrong in school, my parents would deduct thirty minutes from my bedtime, so I wouldn't be able to see all of *90210*.

How could you do that to a kid? Whose parents let their child watch half of a show? I mean, c'mon. If you're going to take away bedtime minutes, take away the whole hour and let me go to bed sometime after dinner; don't tease me with half pleasures! It was ridiculous.

To combat that, I would go to the bus stop in the morning and talk to the parents that waited in their cars to see their kids get on the bus and ask them if they saw the show last night. I'd get all the information from them, and then I could go into school and wow the girls with my *adult* analysis of what was happening in Beverly Hills. Of course, they wanted to go out on a date with me to see a movie or hang out after school sometime, but of course that *privilege* had been taken away from me before it was ever given! Come to think about it, I don't think my mother and stepfather *ever* let me go on a date. It's a known fact that if you tell your kid no, he or she will want to do it anyways. That in itself, explains a lot about what I've done in my life.

One particular day during another glorious attempt to learn math, Mrs. Poxiloni handed me the results of the latest math test. I scored higher on this one than I thought I would have, but even if you added together the score I received with the score I *thought* I would receive, I still would have failed. As with most tests that score that low, a parental signature was required to provide the teacher with the parents' acknowledgment of how their child performed on the test. Well, there was no freakin' way I was going to bring home this incriminating piece of evidence, let alone have my parents sign it. Oh no, forget that idea!

Unfortunately, Mrs. P. was very persistent in getting that paper signed and she would ask me every single day for it. She was relentless. I started to dislike her a little. As each day passed, I would come up with a new excuse for why I didn't have the paper signed. I can't tell you how many of our family pets had to die during the course of my lies. I even showed tears to support my claim that we lost another member of the family.

At one point, Mrs. P. was growing noticeably tired of all the funerals I was attending, and she said that if I didn't bring in the signed paper by tomorrow morning, she was going to call my parents and let them know what was going on. My body froze up. I knew that I was going to have to find a way to figure this whole thing out. Meanwhile, Halloween was right around the corner, and it was one of my favorite times of the year. I never really liked to get all dressed up, but I *did* love the candies....

That day I when I went home, I thought of just going right up to my mother and telling her a grandiose story consisting of a teacher that had it in for me. As much of a good idea as that could have been, there were two problems with it:

1. I was pretty sure I had used that excuse before.

And

2. I liked Mrs. P.

So, what's a kid to do when he decides not to lie to his mother, but still needs to get her signature on a piece of paper that screams her son is an idiot? Well, he signs it for her. And that's just what I did. I felt good about the felonious act of forgery that I had just committed, because in my professional opinion, the signature matched my mother's perfectly. I would soon learn, after handing in the signed document, that I was wrong, and my attempt to help my mother out by signing her name was not going to fly. Like many times before, a phone call was made.

The punishment on this latest criminal act was one that I'll never forget. My stepfather and mother took away Halloween! I couldn't freakin' believe it. How the hell can a parent take away Halloween from a kid like that? If I'd had any aptitude for art, then signing my mother's signature would have been met with sincere congratulations, but *no*, I wasn't blessed with that gift. Thanks a lot, God. To add insult to injury, they grounded me to my room that night, and I sat there staring out the window at all the kids who were walking around trick-or-treating without me.

I've been punished most of my life for the mistakes that I've made, but luckily enough I don't have a good memory when it comes to what I've had to endure because of those mistakes. This situation was different back then, and it would stay different to this day. I will never forget that punishment. I will never forget that *privilege* that they took away from me.

16

FLASH GORDON

The school year was moving forward at a relatively acceptable speed, but I couldn't quite find my place in the school. I tried a number of different ideas to gain some sort of acceptance, but nothing was really taking. I played basketball with the athletic kids and never shot the ball. Instead, I always passed it to them so they could make the shot and be the heroes. When I got tired of doing that, I tried talking to the kids that loved academics. I even picked up an *Encyclopedia Britannica* and read everything there was to read about aardvarks. Unfortunately, it was a gigantic waste of time, because even the nerdy kids don't give a shit about aardvarks. I also tried to hang out with the girls during recess, playing hopscotch and jump-rope. I started to get a little bit of attention, but unfortunately, it wasn't from the girls. Instead, it was from a kid by the name of Dylan Twinkleton. Obviously that wasn't the kind of attention I was looking for, and after Twinkleton violated my personal space by trying to jump-rope with me, using my rope at the same time I was using it, I decided to put an end to that.

The last thing I tried went against everything that I believed in. I was desperate now, and I needed to take drastic measures: I needed to learn multiplication! I remembered that last year

Timmy Tilapovich would just shout out the answer when a flash card was shown, and the kids loved him for that. Now they would love me.

We had a different teacher for math class, and our class would go to her classroom to learn math, and her class would come to ours so Mr. Lurchel could teach them English. I never understood why that was, but I didn't make the rules, so who cares.

My math teacher was a really nice lady. I remember that she had really thick, dark hair, and a pretty rough complexion. Her name was Mrs. Paulina Poxiloni, and she was a very soft-spoken woman who seemed to really care about her students. I liked that about her. What I didn't like all that much was the disgusting stained coffee mug that she always had on the cabinet behind her desk. It was gross and it stunk! The crazy thing about that mug was how proud she was of it. On the front of the cup, it read "30. Over the hill." I didn't understand how someone could be proud of that. It was as if she'd reached a milestone in life, and the whole world needed to know about it. I honestly never gave a shit about the coffee mug; all I cared about was finding some way to learn those damn *x*'s.

Now, in order for me to become really good at multiplication, I needed to get my hands on some of those flashcards. I visually scanned the room until I spotted my mathematical treasure sitting on Mrs. Poxiloni's desk. I would need to somehow find a way to get those home.

At the end of the day, I walked back over to Mrs. P.'s class and saw her sitting at her desk. When she saw me, she smiled, and I walked over to her. She said, "Hi, Jason, is there something I can help you with?"

I said, "No, I just wanted to say goodbye." I was stalling, trying to buy enough time to figure out how I was going to be able to take the cards off her desk.

She said, "Oh, okay, well goodbye, Jason; I'll see you tomorrow during math class."

She then put her head down and went back to grading papers. I stood there disappointed in myself for not being able to figure out how to pull of this heist. My stomach started to turn, and I realized that the smell from her freshly poured cup of coffee was making me sick. Then, as if someone turned on a light in the space between my ears, I knew just what to do.

I said, "Hey, Mrs. Poxiloni, where did you get that coffee mug? I really like it." She quickly raised her head, and the smile she shot me went from ear to ear. She was like a real-life version of one of those, "I'm the proud parent of an honor-roll student" bumper stickers!

She said, "Thank you, Jason," and then turned to get the coffee mug, and at that moment, I swiped the flashcards and tucked them into my faux-Skid pants' waistband. I did it, and I got away with it. The only problem was now I had to listen to a story so long and detailed about how she acquired the mug that I almost missed my bus. I thought it would never end. She just kept yapping and yapping about something to do with a vacation she went on a couple of years ago. There was a birthday and a party and some mention about skiing and a mechanical bull. I didn't know what the hell she was talking about, and I didn't give a shit because with each passing moment, the flashcards kept trying to escape my pants. I stood there in front of Ms. Talks-a-Lot, repeatedly adjusting my crotch so the pack of cards wouldn't fall out the bottom of my pant leg. When she finally shut that hole in her mouth, I did one last adjustment and thanked her for her time.

When I got home that day, I quickly ran to my room, shut the door, and hopped on my bed. I pulled out the flashcards and just stared at them. This was it. I was going to learn this, and there was nothing stopping me.

I flipped through those flashcards until one of the siblings yelled, "Dinner!" I went downstairs, ate, and then went right back upstairs for more time with the cards. I remember having this feeling of ambition. I had never felt that before. It was as if I wanted to learn. I wanted to accomplish something.

I worked on those flashcards late into the night, until I knew multiplication from front to back and could speak it as if it was my first language. I was so proud of what I'd been able to accomplish.

I was able to learn something by myself in a few hours that I couldn't learn in school in a year and a half.

The next day when we got to school and everyone was playing on the blacktop waiting for the morning bell to ring, I snuck inside the building and walked over to Mrs. Poxiloni's class. I was hoping that the door was unlocked, and I held my breath as I turned the handle. With a click, the door popped open, and I walked inside. I took the box of flashcards out of my backpack and walked over to her desk. I had originally planned on putting the cards back on her desk. However, as I was about to do that, the devil horns came out of my head, and instead, I turned around, walked over to Stumpit's desk, and put the cards inside it.

I ran back outside and waited for the bell to ring. When it did, we all went inside and started our day. Like an evil mastermind, I waited to see what would happen when Mrs. Poxiloni noticed her flashcards were missing. Minutes passed that felt like hours, and eventually there was a tap on the door. I looked over to see a big head of dark hair standing there. It was Mrs. P! I was so excited. Mr. Lurchel yelled for her to enter the room. She walked over to Gordy, but instead of stopping at his desk and beating him up for stealing the cards, she walked right past him and stopped at my desk. She asked Lurchel for permission to speak with me for a minute in the hall way. He said yes and we walked out of the room.

I stood there in the hallway staring up at her, nervous about what she was going to say. After what seemed like days of silence, she finally spoke and said, "Jason, I noticed that you took the flashcards off my desk yesterday, and I didn't want to say anything, because I was applauding your desire to learn, but can you tell me why I found them in Gordon's desk this morning?"

I couldn't believe it! I was positive that I had gotten away with it without being detected! I was so sure that my attempt to frame Gordon for the theft of the cards had worked. How could this have happened? Quickly weighing my options, I answered her question the only way I knew how. I said, "I don't know."

She stood there staring at me. She clearly knew that I took the cards, but I wasn't willing to admit to it. I figured that there was going to be a phone call made to my parents, and I was going to get into more trouble. As a young kid, that's the worst feeling.

Seeing the fear in my eyes, Mrs. Poxiloni put her hand on my shoulder and said, "Okay Jason … well, the next time you need something, just ask me." I said okay and she walked away.

Later that day during math class, we played a multiplication flashcard game, and I ended up winning. I should have been thrilled about being the "King of the times tables," but there was an uneasy feeling in my stomach, and I couldn't figure out why it was there.

I learned later in life that feeling was one I had most days growing up with my parents. It was fear, and it was a feeling that was predicated by the living environment that my parents developed. I learned through my experiences that if a parent physically or threateningly disciplines their kid every time he or she does something wrong instead of positively reinforcing the mistake,(such as sitting their child down and explaining the bad they've done in a more upbeat, positive manner),that kid will grow up scared of his parents instead of respecting them.

I had become that kid. At some point in my life, I had developed an inability to avoid making horrible decisions. I understood the difference between right and wrong, but something continued to draw me closer to the side of error. As odd as it might seem, I had become so afraid of what punishment I would get if I did something wrong, I would just do something wrong to find out what the punishment was in order to get it over with. It was a destructive lifestyle that I would grow to hate, but not have the ability to stop.

17

CRY WOLF

With the multiplication situation all taken care of, I started to have a new fond feeling for school. I felt that anything was possible. My relationship with Mr. Lurchel had started to heal itself, and although Gordy and I never really became the best of friends, we were able to put up with each other. I also think that what turned the tables around for me that second year in fourth grade had to do with a certain movie by the name of, *Glory*. It was a movie about the Civil War and the first black regiment to fight for the North. *Glory* was really bloody and packed with a star-studded cast that made the film exciting to watch. All that said, what I liked most about it was the fact that it was rated R. You can't beat that. A fourth grader watching an R-rated movie in school during a time where people thought that *The Simpsons* should be banned. Life doesn't get any better.

Hanging out with different people during recess also helped me become a better student. I've always been the type of person who looks for acceptance, and it doesn't matter if I'm good at something or not; without that acceptance, I can't focus very well. I need to know that no matter what, there's someone out there rooting for me. Playing a sport I wasn't crazy about or reading something I didn't want to read was a desperate attempt to steal that acceptance instead of it coming naturally. But I'd given that up and was spending as much time doing things that made me happy. I found a group of guys that liked to play football at recess, so we did that. And the most surprising thing I learned about myself that year … I loved multiplication! We had made up, and I wanted to spend the rest of my life with her.

One day during math class, Mrs. Poxiloni handed out a piece of paper that didn't look like multiplication to me at all. It had something different on it. It was a weird foreign shape. It was alien. And I wasn't quite sure I liked what was going on. Being the new, highly regarded member to the world of mathematics, my hand shot up in the air like a little Nazi soldier.

Mrs. Poxiloni said, "Yes Jason, I thought you'd raise your hand. What can I help you with?"

I said, "Well, Mrs. P., there seems to be a shape on this paper I'm unfamiliar with."

She replied, "Yes, Jason, it's called *division*."

I was taken aback by that comment and felt myself get offended by her knowledge of this so called *division*. There was no mention of this before, and I didn't remember reading about it in the back of my book that I skimmed through at the beginning of the year. Something was amiss. I needed to find out as much as I could about this *division* thing before I found myself hating it to the point that it would take me over a year and a half to learn it.

Mrs. P. went up to the front of the room and wrote the division symbol down on the board.

Even though I saw what it looked like on the paper that was sitting in front of me, I couldn't quite see what was on the board, so I walked to the front of the room and stood next to Mrs. Poxiloni.

She said, "Jason, please take your seat."

I said, "I can't right now, Paulina, I'm having a hard time seeing the board where I'm sitting."

She immediately stopped what she was doing to shoot a look at me that said, "If you ever call me by my first name again, I'm going to divide your brain from your head."

I understood the math right away, apologized, and went back to my seat. That was the first time I realized that teachers didn't want to be called by their first names. I didn't agree with it, because I thought she had a beautiful name.

All right, back to math. Now, I'm not going to say that I didn't like the way that the division symbol looked, because I did. A dot, a line, and another dot? C'mon, that's a recipe for success. What confused me about it all was whether we needed it or not. I remember that year being the first year that I started to really remember football stats for my New York Jets, and I wasn't sure I had a whole lot of room left in my memory to take on another math symbol. We had a symbol to subtract something; we had a symbol to add something; and we had a symbol to multiply something. What more did we really need?

Mrs. P. would immediately answer that question when she said, "Okay class, in case you're wondering, *division* is the opposite of multiplication. My eyes went from the paper I was looking at in front of me right up to Paulina, I mean Mrs. Poxiloni. The opposite? What did she mean by that? It sounded really confusing, and I knew that I was going to need to find out what the hell was going on.

Mrs. P. went over the basics of division on the board, but I couldn't see what she was doing, so when the bell rang to end class, I walked up to her and asked her if I could move my seat to the front of the room. She sighed and said yes. It seemed she was still angry about me calling her Paulina, but I didn't care. I needed to learn this stuff, and that's all that mattered.

The next day, I was sitting in the front of the room and still squinting to see the board. I could tell that Mrs. P. started to get a little worried about my obsessive squinting, and before I knew it, there was a phone call made to my mother telling her that she should look into getting me glasses. I wish I could have been a fly on that wall, because I could picture the untrusting smile start to form on my mother's face as she would probably tell Mrs. P. that she would look into it as soon as possible.

I can't tell you that my mother jumped at the opportunity to get embarrassed again in front of another optometrist. What I can tell you, is that I eventually got a second chance to take an eye test and would finally get to wear glasses for the first time … that next spring.

18

Happy Birthday

I started to become friends with more and more people, and I really think that it had a lot to do with the new-found academic confidence that I had in myself. My grades started to improve a little, and I noticed that a couple of the girlies were checkin' out my goods. One of them in particular was a thicker girl by the name of Roshanda Williams. She was a nice person and never had a mean word to say to me. I liked her enough to consider sharing a cupcake with her, but I didn't look at her in a way that would make me want to give her half of my bologna sandwich, if you know what I'm saying. What I remember the most about Roshanda was the invite she gave me to attend her all-girl birthday party. I was the only boy invited, and it felt pretty cool to have that much power. I told her that I would try to make it.

When I was given permission to attend the birthday party, I was super excited. I liked girls back then. I liked them a lot. And although the infamous first kiss hadn't happened yet, I knew that it couldn't be too far away.[2]

When I got to the party at Roshanda's house, there were at least ten girls. I walked in there with enough confidence that one

---

[2] I hope I'm not sounding like the girl from *Dear God, It's Me, Margaret.*

hearing of the story would assume I was wearing a white leisure suit. I loved the attention, and when you're a boy at an all-girl party, you get a lot of it. Especially when it comes down to hitting the piñata. Let me tell ya, diamonds might be a girl's best friend when you get older, but candy is like diamonds to them when they're younger. They acted like vultures and were begging me to split open that hanging sugar emporium.

I stepped up in front of it with bat in hand, resting the bat over my shoulder like I was freakin' Joe DiMaggio posing for a baseball card photo. I looked around the room, smiling as cockily as I possibly could. As I went from girl to girl displaying the one and a half inchdimples that say, "Hey, baby, I'm Jase …" They all smiled back even bigger. When I got to Roshanda, I winked, blew her a kiss, and saw her legs buckle as she almost fainted.

I got into a batter's stance and warmed up by taking a couple of practice swings. When I was ready, I choked up on the bat a little and swung as hard as I possibly could …

Strike one!

I laughed and naturally said, "Just kidding," as I started my practice swings again. I closed my eyes, trying to concentrate harder. I started to imagine what it would be like to be a starting player for the New York Yankees.[3] When I opened my eyes, I was ready to win the game for the Yanks. I stepped, swung, and whacked that Mexican papier-mâché with prejudice! Unfortunately, it swung forward, backward, to the side, and then rested back in the spot it started in.

Foul ball, strike two!

I started to sweat a little. I noticed that the girls in the room had begun to lose a little faith in my ability to get them what they really wanted. That made me very angry, and I could feel the stomach fire starting to smoke. I couldn't let this thing beat me. My future as a ladies man was at stake.

When it was time to try again, I knew this was my last shot. I gripped the bat as hard as I could, lined up my swing with the target, and swung with the strength of an eighth grader. The

---

[3] Hey, don't hate me; this is my dream, not yours.

piñata busted open before it went flying across the room and almost hit two girls in the face as it flew into a lamp and shattered it. I didn't have time to say I was sorry, because the girls scattered like the four winds in a desperate attempt to snatch up as much candy as they could possibly hold.

I stood there watching what seemed to resemble a pride of lionesses feasting on their latest kill. I was hoping one of them might look up and thank me for all my hard work, but nope, not even Roshanda. At that moment, it became quite clear to me that Roshanda didn't like me because I was good looking; she was just using me to break open her stupid piñata.

The rest of the party sucked. We just stood around and played board games and combed Barbie's hair. I never liked Barbie—*or* Ken, for that matter—and couldn't understand how the hair of a plastic doll could get messy enough to have a party in which you feel the need to comb it. I don't know what Roshanda was doing with her dolls, but something wasn't right.

When it was time to go, I said goodbye to my gracious hosts, and after receiving my goody bag that didn't consist of *any* of the piñata candy, I headed out the door. It had felt really good being invited to a party like that, but it left me feeling kind of empty. I don't know why, but I remember feeling used and alone. I remember wondering if those girls hated me now. They must hate me after I broke that lamp. I decided from that moment on that I wouldn't attend anymore all-girl parties.

19

No Mas Numero Quatro

The really cool part about being friends with Roshanda was that, through her, I was able to meet Kerry Kissinger. She was a really short girl, even for the fourth grade, but had a delightfully sweet demeanor. Her pimp of a friend, Roshanda, felt that Kerry and I would make a great couple and set the whole thing up. I was really excited, but a little nervous about it because Kerry had a reputation for liking to lock lips as often as possible. I remembered what it was like the first time I went through this, and I wasn't all about going through that again, but I didn't have much of a choice. Kerry was a bit of a first-base whore, and I knew I would eventually have to step up to the plate.

Every day after school, the kids would line up against the wall to wait for the bus to arrive, and after being Kerry's boyfriend for a fourth-grade record of three and a half days, the pressure was building to give Kerry a taste of the ol' Italian Stallion lips. I needed to get this over with, so after the final bell rang, I made up my mind to do this thing.

As I walked over to where I knew Kerry would be waiting for the bus, my heart started pounding. I was a man on a mission, and I had an idea of how I would softly lay my lips to hers, but as I got closer, I realized that I was walking faster and faster. My

89

heart pounded harder and harder. She saw me walking toward her and stood up knowing that this was going to be our big moment. When I got to her, I grabbed her shirt as if she owed me money, pulled her into me, and as I was about to make history, I must've puckered up inside out because instead of kissing her squarely on the lips, I bit my own! As I winced in pain, I dropped my head a little, and she ended up kissing my nose.

Naturally, there was an awkward silence, and then I heard laughter. I looked up to see three kids standing there pointing at me, and before I could tell them to leave me alone, I heard Mr. Lurchel yell from behind me, "Jason, we don't do that here. I want two pages written tonight on how you won't kiss girls in the hallway." I couldn't believe it! My first kiss comprised years and years of anxiety, a racing heart, horrible adrenaline, assault, personal injury, and embarrassment. Now, to top it all off, I had to write a punishment assignment. Oh, the humanity!

When I got home that day, I felt like shit. It seemed that I couldn't do anything right. I remember lying in bed after dinner crying for hours. I knew that getting embarrassed and having a hard time in school had a lot to do with it, but it just didn't seem right that I was that depressed. I wanted to find out why, but I didn't know where to look, and I was afraid to ask anyone. So I got out of bed, did my homework, and completed my punishment assignment by writing, "I will not bite my own lip and get kissed on the nose again. I will not bite my own lip and get kissed on the nose again …" It was not the exact way that Lurchel wanted it, but I didn't give a shit.

My relationship with Kerry lasted another week, because we had gotten to the point that we were sneaking kisses without the teacher looking and every time we did it, I'd somehow bite my lip. The pain started to get a little too much to bear, so I told Kerry that I couldn't be her boyfriend anymore, because my lips were getting in the way of us really getting to know each other. I thought that she was going to get upset over it, but to my surprise, she just shrugged her shoulders, said okay and walked away.

❖❖❖

With fourth grade coming to a close, I stayed as far away from girls as I could. I wanted to make sure that I would pass this time, so I focused as hard as possible on that. The hard work paid off, and with the final report card in my hand confirming the success of the infamous fourth grade, I went home. I always got excited about the end of the year, because I'd have time off from school, but the excitement leaned more toward getting to see Pop and Darling and the Jersey Shore. This particular year, the excitement was divided: I had accomplished what I set out to do, and I would go through the entire summer without giving the fourth grade another thought.

20

JOHNNY NUMBER 5

F
ifth grade was a big deal to me. In Torrington, Connecticut, fifth grade was the end of elementary school because sixth grade was the start of junior high school. Being able to call myself a fifth-grader might have been advantageous, because it meant I was the big boy on campus. But that amount of power could be dangerous for someone like me. I was always willing to show that I had no problem acting out to gain attention, but being in a position of authority, as one of the oldest kids in the school, was a situation that could even be disastrous. I knew that I would really need to focus on not acting like a fool, especially considering that my parents' punishments were becoming more and more creative, and I was not about to give up another childhood holiday. Last year, it was Halloween, and I would not be surprised if they tried to take away Easter this year! What would Jesus think?

My fifth-grade teacher's name was Mrs. Shirley P. Littlefoot. She was a very short lady with awkwardly curly hair and an underbite resembling the English bulldog I've wanted my entire life. She was also the leader of a group of ninja assassins that killed people with throwing-knives shaped like the symbol for π. No, I'm just kidding, but now that I have your attention, she *was* the leader of a hand-selected group of kids referred to as T.A.G. which stood for Talented and Gifted.

Mrs. Littlefoot had tried to recruit me into TAG once last year, because during a test of historical knowledge, she observed, it seemed, that I knew all the answers, and if it wasn't for Stumpit's ridiculous ability to absorb useless information, I would have won! What Mrs. Littlefoot didn't realize until later was that I didn't really know the answers. For weeks leading up to the competition, I kept getting the questions wrong and somehow, I developed the ability to memorize something through the embarrassment of not knowing it. Mrs. L. just happened to see me in action after many weeks of embarrassment. She was very excited about me at first (*last* year), but that was short-lived. When she got me in a room alone to go over a new set of questions and I didn't know *any* of the answers, she quickly changed her mind. I thought I even saw tears forming in her eyes as her hopes of having someone as attractive as me leading her team to victory drifted off like a lonely cloud looking for the family it thought it once had.

So, *this* year, I'm sure she was unpleasantly surprised the day she received the student roster with my name on it, reminding her that her recruiting skills weren't as good as they once were. I could feel the tension in the room, so as soon as I could, I walked over to her and introduced myself as if we had never met before. She shook my hand and shot me a quizzical look, probably wondering if I had lost my damn mind, but I didn't care.

She said, "Um, nice to meet you, Jason, now please take your seat." I walked back over to the tiny wooden desk with my name card neatly placed on the top and sat down. As first days always go, the teacher would give a grand introduction and then go over what we were to learn that year. Mrs. L. walked up to the front of the room—I remember hearing her shoes clapping on the floor twice as many times as a normal-sized teacher's feet would. She finally got to the front of the room, and there I was, right in the front with my head in my hands gleaming up at her. It took her quite a few tries to get out the simple words to form an introduction. She was probably wondering what the hell I was staring at.

This year was a little harder than the year before, because we would have to switch classes twice instead of just once. That's a big switch for a kid. If I was good at math, I might say that was a 100 percent increase from the year before! However, I'm not good at math, so let's just say I thought fifth grade was going to be harder.

I understood the reason to increase the number of classes we'd have to switch: because in sixth grade, we would have a different classroom for *every* class. I remember feeling a sense of appreciation for the school in helping to prepare the students for what would happen the following year. Unfortunately, fifth grade would be the last year that I felt schools prepared students for things to expect.

So, there we were: fifth-graders. The top of the school. The cream of the crop. My balls hadn't dropped yet, but it didn't matter because when you're a fifth grader, you're the man! We had a different class for Math *and* Social Studies, and I started to feel a sense of responsibility. I'm not saying that I liked the feeling, but it was there. I knew that this was going to be a special year. I knew Multiplication; I knew Division. Nothing was going to stop me from making this year the best academic year of my short academic life. I was ready! Nobody could deter me from Excellence. I sat there that first day in Math class feeling like I was King of a Castle! That is, until my Kingdom was invaded when we were informed that we'd be learning something referred to as *Long Division*. My heart hit my sneakers. I thought that Division took long enough, and I was not happy about this latest mathematical development. My mind went from Euphoric Academia to Mental Frustration in mere seconds. My heart started racing; I wanted to cry. I wanted to run out of the building. Sweat formed on my brow, and I felt like I was going to be sick. A minute ago, I was happy and excited about this new year, and now I felt the opposite. That instant fall into depressive feelings would be another red flag that I would choose to ignore, because I wasn't educated enough to understand that it wasn't normal.

21

Take That

Two things you should know about me: The first thing is that I never liked to eat fish sticks, and whenever my mother made them for dinner, I would *always* find a way to get out of eating them. The second thing is that I was never a horribly accident-prone kid growing up. You never saw me hobbling around on crutches trying to nurse a broken leg. You never saw me with a bunch of "get-well" signatures on a gigantic cast from falling out of a tree.

One time, I *did* get a small paper cut on my pointer finger, and after wrapping it with half a roll of toilet paper and a full roll of scotch tape, I tried to convince people that I had broken it and would have to wear my finger cast for at least two days. While I was telling the horrific tale of the finger break, a crowd started to form around me and some of the students seemed very concerned, but Mrs. Littlefoot wasn't buying it. She told me that if I was that hurt, then maybe she should call my parents and let them know about my injury. I had to make an executive decision, so I ripped off my makeshift finger cast, threw my hands up in the air, and yelled, "It's a miracle!"

Mrs. L. just stood there staring at me as if she were Sméagol and I, Frodo Baggins wearing the ring that she wanted so badly. It was creepy, to say the least.

After school that day, I was completely healed from my traumatic run-in with the imaginary finger break, and it was time to go play outside. I got a couple of my friends together, and we decided to play a game rightfully named, Guns. The idea of the game was to capture the bad guy. One team would be the police and the other team would be the outlaws. Of course, we all fought to be the police because they are just so cool when you're in fifth grade. Funny how things turn around as you get older ...

My partner, TJ Starsky, who lived one block away on 21 Jump Street, would be my partner for this game. We obviously didn't use real guns or even BB guns, for that matter. Come to think about it, we didn't even put caps in our guns, because no one could really afford them. As dumb as it sounds, I have to be honest and say that we spent most of our time running around, shooting each other by making vocal noises of what a gun was *supposed* to sound like, and then arguing about who shot who first. I would rather have used real guns.

This particular day was a little different from normal Gun days, because we decided to play it on one of the gigantic dirt mountains left at one of the home-construction sites. We'd received word that our suspect was in the area and we were to proceed with caution, because he was listed as armed and dangerous. My partner looked at me and asked if I was ready, and in my best impression of Sylvester Stallone, I said, "Let's do this!" We set off on our manhunt. The suspect, Donny John Demarco, was wanted in connection with the humiliation he'd caused by telling everyone that I had a third nipple. He was also wanted for illegal sales and distribution of coffee beans to minors. He would pay for his crimes, and I was the man to bring him to justice.

Starsky and I started to climb the dirt mountain in hopes of running into Donny, and as we reached the summit, we heard, "Bang bang, I got you!"

In unison, TJ and I both yelled, "Fuck you, you missed!" Then it was all on. I told TJ to go around the side of the mountain and get behind his position. I laid suppressive fire as I started to fire bullets from both my guns for at least ten minutes, until Demarco pointed out how unfair that was because I only had one gun. I thought about it, apologized, and told him to give up because he was surrounded.

After a few seconds of silence, I sent over another couple of bang bangs, and he said, "Okay, I give up, stop shooting!"

I smiled as I slowly stood up to see that Demarco had thrown his gun down and was standing there behind a large mud puddle with his arms behind his head waiting to get taken to jail. I slowly started my decent down the side of the mountain, and as I got closer, I saw TJ finally getting into a position behind Demarco and holding him at gunpoint. Because this particular terrain was weak at best, I quickly lost my footing and found myself sliding down the side of the mountain barreling toward the suspect, my partner, and the gigantic mud puddle. In order to prevent myself from rolling into the pool of wet dirt, I brought my knee up to stop myself in a last desperate attempt to prevent my clothes from getting wet and ended up whacking myself in the mouth.

Blood immediately shot out from my mouth along with a good chunk of my lip. I lay there for a couple of seconds, not truly understanding the severity of this injury. I knew that my mouth didn't feel that good, but I didn't realize that it was missing part of itself.

Picking myself up off the ground, I assured my friends that the game was over and my team had won, before I made my way home to tell my mother that I had a boo-boo. When I got there, the news of the simple injury was taken with a little more seriousness than I thought it deserved, and I was taken to the hospital to receive something called Stitches. I didn't like the sound of that as I sat in the waiting room imagining some doctor making a sweater out of my face.

A few hours and three stitches later, my mother took me home and fed me and my numb mouth some fish sticks. My mother was always a smart woman and those fish sticks were delicious.

22

No Evidence

Long division proved to be very time-consuming and I was *not* a big fan of the whole process. I promised myself that when I got old enough, I would buy the most expensive calculator on the market. I would show them. Sure, I'd listen to them now, but when I got out of there, there'd be no long division for me ... *ever*!

Fifth grade started rolling by at a pretty fast pace and that pleased me. The teachers kept things moving along through activities that I hadn't experienced before. My history teacher in particular was a woman who did things outside of the typical realm of normalcy. Her name was Ms. Alexandria Almanac. She was very knowledgeable in many subjects, and I liked that because it seemed like she had passion in what she did instead of just learning the material she would teach.

Ms. Almanac would host a lip-synching talent show every year based on songs from a certain era. We were all asked to branch off into groups, and a couple of times a week, instead of learning *History*, we would have to practice our songs. It was awesome! This was the single best thing I got a chance to do in school. I was in a group with three lucky ladies, and I was the lip-synching lead vocalist. How sweet is that? If I remember correctly, I was the most talented lip-syncher in that school, and I couldn't wait to show off my talents.

We didn't come up with a group name, but the talent I possessed was enough to get away with having a musical group with no name. The only thing holding me back from giving the greatest performance in fifth-grade lip-synching *history,* was my focus during rehearsals. Simply put, I didn't have any. I couldn't concentrate to save my life, and the reason for that was one of my backup dancers.

Her name was Elizabeth Brewer, and she made me more nervous than a crack-head at a police convention. At that point in my life, I had already survived my first overdose; run away from home; almost been murdered with a hammer; survived a parental divorce, my stepfather's disciplinary style, and daily academic humiliation. I assumed that there wasn't anything else that could shake me up, but boy was I wrong. There was just something about Liz Brewer that made me forget whatever it was I was going to say every time I was around her.

During those couple of weekly rehearsal opportunities, Liz and the other girls in the group (McKenzie Sparks and Jennifer Godburn) would ask me to join them in going over the dance moves that Liz herself was choreographing. As much as I loved the attention back then, it was just hard to stand near Liz without feeling like I was going to faint, so I would regularly come up with excuses for why I couldn't rehearse. I assured them that when the curtain went up, I'd be ready. That seemed to be enough to keep them off my back. Many weeks later, the day had arrived for me to break out of my shell and show the world that I was the reason Michael Jackson moves the way he does. I was ready. I had no idea how I was going to pull off the performance of a lifetime, but I didn't care.

The morning of the performance yielded minor butterflies in the pit of my stomach, and not even the generic cereal my mother purchased was going to scare them away. I skipped breakfast, grabbed my books for school, and after hearing that no one in my family would be attending the talent show, I stepped out the door and walked to the bus stop. I remember feeling a little disappointed that I wouldn't have anyone in my corner rooting me on like I was sure the other parents were going to do for their kids, but I wouldn't let that deter me. I was a performer now, and the show had to go on! Besides, my mother said that the teachers were going to be videotaping the show and making copies, so why would she have to go? Right?

When I got to school, I saw Liz walking up to me in the hallway. She walked with a certain confidence about her, and I always admired that. She said, "Good morning, are you ready to do this?" Now, on any other day with any other girl, I would have replied with, "Ready? I was BORN ready!" That being the catch phrase of the 80s that I couldn't let go of. Unfortunately, this wasn't an ordinary girl, this was *Liz Brewer!* I wish I could remember what my response was to the girl I couldn't speak normally around, but I don't. I'm sure it consisted of letters joining together to form words that haven't been invented yet. I was a barely functioning retarded person around her, and she didn't seem to mind. That of course made me act *more* retarded.

We all assembled in the cafeteria where the show would be held, and waited in our prospective groups to be called to the front. The room was filled with the excitement of fifth-grade children and the pride parents feel when building their own kid up and bragging about them to the parent next to them as if their kid was better. I sat there looking around the room witnessing that and feeling very jealous. I knew that my parents loved me, but it just seemed to me that they had a different way of showing it. In fifth grade, you want your parents at *every* function, no matter how big or small it is. That's the only thing a kid at that age really wants. Forget the toys and the fun vacations, he just wants loving recognition. That day, I didn't get what I wanted.

When our group was announced as Jason's Group, I hopped off the chair and walked slowly to the front of the room. This was my time to shine, and I wanted to take as much of it as I could. I took my unrehearsed position in the front of the group with my three back-up dancers behind me, and put my head down in preparation for the music to start. Seconds later, the first few notes of "California Dreaming" by the Mamas and the Papas started to play, which made my right knee start to move back and forth as my arms slowly extended out to the sides. I seductively lifted my head slowly to face my audience, and when it was time, I opened my mouth and lip-synched the shit out of that song! I was moving around that make-believe stage in the front of the cafeteria as if I owned the building, the building next to it, and the bank down the road from it! A few minutes later, the music slowed to a stop, the audience roared to an explosive applause, and the show was over.

I felt alive! They loved me, they really, really loved me! I was on top of the world and adored by all that were there. Well, at least for the next five minutes. Apparently, in fifth-grade show business, you're only popular from the time you take the stage to the time the next act takes it.

About a week later, I was given the tape from the talent show to take home for my mother to view. As she sat there and watched it, she made many comments on the outfits and early development of fifth-grade girls at that time, and that's all I remember her saying. I'm more than confident that she complimented me on my performance, but it wasn't in a way that evokes a confident memory. Looking back on my life now, I don't ever remember a time in which my mother was jumping up and down with joy over anything I've accomplished. I've always wondered if that was because she just showed excitement differently or if I've never done something worthy of the more dramatic display.

As for the videotaped evidence of the greatest performance in fifth-grade lip-synching history … it's gone, and I blame that on the beauty and talent of Mariah Carey. Later that year, she was on an award show singing her song "Hero," and I taped over my only video-captured elementary performance to tape something that had no real significant value on fifth-grade or US history. Damn you, Mariah Carey, and your amazing voice and marketable good looks!

23

I FELT THAT ONE

The really great part about being a kid growing up on the East Coast was the snow. I will stand by my feelings that, aside from the ocean, snow *has* to be the most exciting thing for a kid to see. There's nothing bad about it *at all!* It keeps you out of school, reminds you that Christmas is close, and gives you an opportunity to go sledding! Snow is just awesome, and there's no other way of looking at it.

My brother Jamie used to wake me up really early in the morning, and we would walk downstairs so we could watch the TV to see if our school would be canceled because of the snow. What a grand celebration when we found out that we could stay home that day! Followed by a briefing in which my brother would explain to me that we would be going out to shovel the neighbor's driveways. He was always scheming on how we could make some money, and winter time was no different. I was to knock on the neighbors' front doors and sell our driveway-shoveling services. Then we would team up on shoveling the driveway, from which he made more money than I did. Not sure how that ended up happening. I'm sure if you'd ask him, he'd tell you that there exists some sort of big-brother surcharge. It's all bullshit.

One snow day in particular, a couple of my friends and I decided to go sledding down the dirt mountain that was off-limits to any type of childhood activity on account of my latest accident that left me with a scar on my lower lip. Of course, on the other hand, we were kids, and kids do what kids do. In this case, we were going sledding on that mountain, and the abominable snowman himself wouldn't be able to stop us.

Now, the mountain itself had four main sides to it, and we'd always sled down three of them. The fourth side of the mountain was really dangerous, because it had quite a few long drops, as well as construction materials and car parts sticking out of it. Can you guess what side I decided to go down?

Yep, you guessed it. One of my friends said to me, "Betcha won't go down that side," and pointed to the hellish part of the mountain almost guaranteeing its victim's certain death. I wasn't about to be called out like that to use my tail to cover my balls. This was serious. My reputation was on the line, and I told that kid what *any* self-respecting fifth-grader would say: "Oh yeah? Well, watch this." With that, I grabbed my bright orange sled made of only the sturdiest plastic known to anyone in the fifth grade and staggered toward the side of the mountain, expecting to never return.

I peered over the side and started to feel a little sick to my stomach. I wanted to turn around and run all the way home. I wanted to swing open my front door, yell for Mommy, run into her arms, and cry myself to sleep until she could wake me up with a hot cup of cocoa and some chicken noodle soup. But let's face it; I wasn't a fourth-grader anymore. There were higher expectations now, and I needed to do this for my fellow fifth-graders. I needed to do this for all the younger kids that looked up to me wondering and dreaming of what it was like to have the strength of someone on the verge of going off to middle school.

Looking back at my audience, I smirked, threw up the shaka sign and said the only words that were appropriate for this situation. I said, "Cowabunga, dudes." With that, I hopped on the sled, pushed off, and headed down the mountain.

The ride was fairly smooth at first, and just when I started laughing to myself about the ease that was being displayed as my plastic sled glided me down the mountain, something went horribly wrong. Before I knew it, I felt a really big bump, blinked really hard, and when I opened my eyes I was surprised to see that my loyal sled was flying down the mountain without me. I was going down this mountain on my back and felt it appropriate to yell out "*Holy shit!*" as loud as I could. The yell itself was interrupted as I felt a slight pinch to my lower leg. I didn't have time to find out what had happened because I was reaching out to grab anything that would slow my speed. Nothing seemed to work, and time proved to be the only thing that would end that ride.

As my shocked body stopped at the bottom of the mountain, I lay there wondering how the hell something like that could have happened. I knew that we didn't really do our due diligence on surveying the sled course, but I didn't think anything like this could happen to me. I had gone down on a very sturdy plastic sled. Those kinds of sleds are supposed to be safe, aren't they? After several minutes, my friends, who had witnessed the accident, finally made their way over to me. They seemed frantic as they asked me if I was okay. I said yes, but didn't move. My cold body had gone numb from the snow and adrenaline, and I didn't want to move. That of course would change when one of my friends, said, "Holy shit, you're bleeding!"

I instantly remembered the pinch I had felt and reached down to find that something had penetrated my snowsuit, two pairs of jeans, two pairs of sweat pants, two pairs of shorts, and then my leg.

My friends found my disloyal traitor of a sled and, within a matter of minutes, had me on it and were dragging me home. My mother wasn't at home at the time, so they called up one of the neighbors. After looking into the severity of my injury, the neighbor, Mrs. Ambulant, decided to take me to the hospital. When we got there and were eventually guided into a room, we learned that my injury was on my upper thigh, right below my ass cheek. My friends, who investigated the scene, found out that a deep slope on the course I took down the mountain pulled the sled out from underneath me and the pinch I felt was from a jagged piece of muffler that was sticking out from the snow.

My mother and stepfather received word of my accident, and I was given a tetanus shot as they sat in the room, watching me lie face down on the table in nothing but my whitey tighties, as the doctor sewed up my upper leg and ass cheek. That was the last time I went sledding on that part of the mountain and the first time I remember feeling funny about my parents seeing me in my underwear.

24

Paging Doctor Ventre

Going back to school after spending part of the evening in the hospital was the best thing that could happen to a kid. As much as it sucked to have to go through an injury, the attention you got *after* the injury made it … well … worth it. All eyes were on you.

There was nothing wrong with my leg, but naturally I formed a slight limp and spoke slowly and softly when I retold the tale of the sledding accident that almost cost me my life. One girl in my class started crying as I went into detail of my chance with death. Now granted, I *did* embellish a little as I added in the tiny detail of the grizzly bear that tried to attack me as I lay in the snow bleeding to death. I probably could have left that out, but c'mon, how many times can you get cut by a muffler sledding? I needed to exaggerate and milk this story as long as I could.

The interesting thing that came out of this whole situation was realizing that I had been spending an abnormal amount of time in hospitals. I came to the conclusion that I wanted to be a doctor. It was as if all these accidents were happening for a reason—and that reason was life's way of telling me that I needed to prepare myself for a lifetime in the field of medicine. As long as there weren't going to be any grape Tylenols, I was happy with what I wanted to do with the rest of my life.

My class got a chance to go to the computer lab once a week on Fridays and play educational computer games. While everyone else in the room was addicted to Oregon Trail, a game that taught you about survival, strategy, and pace, I always played a game whose object was to put the body parts of a skeleton back in the part of the body they belonged. I mean come on—how many fifth-grade children know where a clavicle is? Not only did I know where it was, but I studied and memorized the overall function of the clavicle—*or collar bone*—and I would talk to people about how it served as support.

As each week passed, I grew more and more excited about becoming a doctor. I didn't care that I was bad at math, and I didn't care that I wasn't a big fan of school. Somehow, someway, I was going to be the next Doogie Howser.

Speaking of careers, my teacher, Mrs. Littlefoot, had requested that each student, every day, invite one of their parents to come speak to the room about what they did for a living. I had asked my stepfather to speak to my class, because he was a cop—and a big one at that. I thought of how good I would look to have someone as intimidating as him come to my school and tell stories.

I sat there that day listening to him speak about his job, and I remember looking at him for the first time with an immense amount of respect for what he did. He didn't have to come speak to my class for me. I could have asked my father to do it, but he was in a different city and let's face it, kids would MUCH rather hear cop stories than stories about a guy closing a big sale. My stepfather really went out of his way to make me look good. I've never forgotten that and will always remember sitting there proud of who he was.

Usually, the parents would come speak to the class for about fifteen minutes or so, but my stepfather was quite the talker and probably stood up there for over an hour, wowing everyone in the room with his stories of chasing bad guys, upholding the law, and protecting the citizens in the great town of Waterbury.

When he left that day, everyone came over to my desk, and I sat there, my face red with pride and happiness. I was shocked that I was getting this much attention, and I hadn't had to go out of my way to get it! I hadn't had to do something outlandish. I hadn't had to lie or cheat. I had just showed off the person my mother chose to marry. It was a really cool feeling, and I've always felt appreciative that he gave that to me.

The only other thing I can say with regard to the fifth grade was that it was the first year I started wearing deodorant. Me and my friend Jimmy Pits would talk about how our parents bought us deodorant, but at the time, we were both lying. Deodorant was cool to us because it was "grown up," and that's what kids nearing middle school want to feel like.

One day, my stepfather took me to the grocery store and let me pick out a deodorant. It was Right Guard, and it smelled fresh and adult, so I chose that one. It was also really tiny, and I thought that was cool-looking as well. Of course, my stepfather would joke about Right Guard and ask me what I was going to put under my left arm. I didn't care that he was making fun that I was growing up. Today it was deodorant; tomorrow it would be a mortgage.

When I got home from the store, I called up Jimmy and told him that we needed to speak immediately, and that it was an emergency. He came right over and I had my mini-deodorant in my pocket as I forced Jimmy to follow me into the basement. I looked at him right in the eyes and said, "Okay, now tell me the truth, are you *really* wearing deodorant?"

He lowered his head in shame and said, "No, are you?"

I whipped out that little deodorant and held it in the air like it was He-Man's sword. I could sense Jimmy's jealousy, but I didn't care. This was my time to shine. I was a man now, and I felt pity for the little boy who was standing in front of me. I told Jimmy that I was very disappointed that he'd lied to me, and then I told him it would be best if he went home. Our friendship had survived a lot at that point, but this was the straw that broke the camels' back. Jimmy and I never spoke to each other again.

Not much else happened during my fifth-grade year. My grades weren't good enough to pass, so I repeated it again a few more times and would eventually start the sixth grade right after my seventeenth birthday. No, seriously, I graduated the fifth grade on time and was really excited about the prospect of becoming a middle school student. What kid wouldn't be? Elementary school is synonymous with *little children*. Middle school students certainly weren't looked at as *adults*, but we weren't little kids anymore. We were growing up, and expectations were set higher now. I remember feeling happy about that.

But first, of course, there would be a summer. What would the end of the year and upcoming beginning of a new year be without mentioning time spent with Pop and Darling in Jersey? No academic success was ever more exciting as it was to pack up our clothes and head off to the shore with them. I knew that I would have to spend as much time enjoying that summer with them, more than I normally did, because next year at school was going to be even more of a challenge than I was used to. As expected, the shore didn't disappoint, and that summer was just as amazing as the all the others preceding it.

25

SIXTH GRADE

The middle school that I attended was called Vogel-Wetmore. "Wetmore" was for the sixth-graders, and "Vogel" was designated for the seventh- and eighth-graders. Once again, I found myself being the low man on the totem pole at a new school. I always enjoyed change, but I hated being looked at as a peon—it always made me feel like I had to do something to prove my self-worth. This school would give me plenty of opportunities to do that.

The school itself was older than Jesus, and there was a rumor out there we would be moving into a brand new school next year—after it was officially built. Until then, I was forced to attend a school that was a little on the decrepit side. What I found most interesting about the school was the lack of a gymnasium. Yeah, I said that: this school didn't have a gym. The students had to walk out of the school and down the road to the YMCA and attend P.E. class there. I had never heard of anything like that before and thought it was simply retarded. The YMCA we attended was also very old, and I never felt safe walking into that building. I'm sure that it was more than structurally sound, but it never gave me a warm and fuzzy feeling.

Gym class had always been my best subject, but sixth-grade gym was quite a bit different. It was a school policy that the students *had* to shower. When I found out about that, I was not completely pleased with the school's decision. I understood that the odor transition from the fifth grade to the sixth grade is quite significant. I remember being able to run around the playground for an hour straight in elementary school without fear of stench, but when you get to middle school, you can sit there just taking a test and smell some nastiness starting to form. However, three things bothered me about this whole *showering with other boys* idea:

1. I didn't like showering with boys.
2. The shower was in the basement of a really old building, and it was kind of creepy being down there.
3. I wasn't as *confident* about what I was working with as I am today. Don't get me wrong, I didn't feel that I resembled a light switch, but at the same time, I didn't play basketball … if you know what I'm saying.

I didn't agree with the school's decision, but you can't fight city hall. I figured that I couldn't be the only boy who felt a little intimidated by this whole naked-shower situation. I found out that we were allowed to wear our bathing suits in the shower, so we didn't have to show our goodies to each other. I just *assumed* that every boy in my class would be wearing them. I was wrong. A couple of kids had mention that they'd better shower naked, because if they didn't, then they would get made fun of. So, after saying that, every boy in that gym class showered naked—except me.

There were two of them who deserve special recognition. One of them was absurdly tall for his age and walked around naked picking his nose, so I never bothered to learn his name, but instead chose to stay away from him. He also liked to sit in the lunch room and hold his breath until his face turned different colors. One day, I witnessed this happening until his face turned a deep shade of blue and a booger popped out of his nose. Then he wiped the booger away and looked around the room to see if anyone was laughing at him. No one dared.

The other kid was short and had curly hair. His name was Dirk Floggle. He liked to take a shower and spend as much time lathering himself up as humanly possible, rinse, and then air dry. That daily routine in itself was one that was highly unacceptable. What made things worse was that he didn't just stand there and air dry by himself, oh no; things couldn't be that easy for me. He decided to strike up conversations with as many people as he could while he stood there with one leg up on the bench rocking back and forth as if he was Captain Morgan. It was freakin' weird, and someone should have stopped him, but what do you say to a naked sixth-grade boy who won't leave you alone?

I knew that the school-enforced all-boy showering would probably scar me for life. So I would spend every day trying to avoid everyone as much as I could. Because of that, my PE grade would suffer. I also found myself getting into arguments with kids really easily, and it was over the dumbest things. There was just something about the stress from being around a bunch of boys in a dimly lit dungeon shower that put me in a bad mood.

After gym one day, I was walking out of the YMCA, and there were two kids leaning up against the railing. For the sake of the story, we will call them Asshole Number One and Asshole Number Two. Asshole Number One was a short kid and Number Two was a big boy.

Number One made a comment as I walked passed him, so I turned around and said, "What'd you say?"

"He said, 'Look—there goes that pansy that isn't even man enough to take a real shower.'"

Now, I'm sure if I thought about it, I could have explained to him that being a man has *nothing* to do with showering with other men, but instead I told him to go fuck himself. His friend, who was now standing behind me, didn't like that, and for some reason reached out and grabbed my book bag. I don't know what he was thinking by doing that, but I let the bag drop off my shoulder and my hands fly up and punch Asshole Number One in the face twice. And then I spun around just in time to see the scared look on Asshole Number Two's face right before I kicked him in the stomach, instantly dropping him to the ground. I picked my backpack up off the ground and walked away.

I sat through that day in school unable to concentrate on anything in fear of my name being called over the intercom inviting me to the principal's office. How would I explain this situation to my parents? I beat up two kids that didn't do anything wrong to me except say a few words I didn't like. I knew that I was wrong for what I did, but I couldn't help it. Something in me went blank, and the ability to fire back with a quick, witty statement was not a possibility. I assaulted two kids without even thinking! That was the first time in my life I remember feeling rage. Feeling a drive that pushed me to do something that I never thought I had the ability to do. I went from zero to sixty without blinking. I knew that if anyone found out about this, I would be suspended. And I was scared to death about it.

Somehow I got through the day without going to the principal's office. The two assholes I beat up didn't tell on me. I couldn't believe it. What I did notice was the next day after gym class, I walked down to the showering area and what I saw brought a large smile to my face. ALL but the two nudist boys were wearing bathing suits in the shower.

26

MIDDLE SCHOOL ROMANCE

Sixth grade typically gives each student the opportunity to grow both emotionally as well as academically. The difference in *dating* from elementary school to middle school was pretty significant. In middle school, when you said that you were "going out" with someone, you were actually expected to "go out" with them. I, of course wasn't allowed to physically go out with anyone, so that left a big challenge for me.

Since the second grade, "dating" was looked at as too adult for me—or used as a target for punishment when I did something wrong. For example, if I got in trouble at school, my parents would, say, extend time to the age that I would be allowed to date. I guess by doing that, they would break up the monotony of the other punishments they were handing down. It's smart when you think about it. I was girl crazy at a young age, and they used that to try to keep me on the straight and narrow. But just remember one thing, parents: if you have a kid like me and you take away the privilege of dating one girl, I'm going to find a way to date ten of them behind your back, so who are you really hurting here?

My first real girlfriend was a short girl by the name of Regina Ferriar. She was fairly new to the Torrington area, and I felt it to be my responsibility to take her under my wing, so to speak. I was attracted to her for the normal reasons any twelve-year-old boy would be attracted to a girl: she was alive and she had boobs. I'm not saying that she didn't have other qualities that made her a fine catch, but those are the two that always stood out to me the most. She also rode on the same bus I rode on, so it made the after-school-bus-riding romance convenient.

Of course, as with most girls, there was a lot about Regina that was left to be desired. Most notably were the shirts that she wore. They were usually collared, button-down shirts, and she somehow managed to usually leave a couple of the top buttons undone, so when we'd ride home on the bus together, my hands would start to sweat, and the embarrassment of that showed on my face. I used to have to hang them out the window as we rode down the road. Another thing that was wrong with her was the constant need to steal kisses from me. Keep in mind, I had siblings that rode on the same bus as I did, and I wasn't supposed to be conversing with the opposite sex, so with Regina always wanting to get kissy-kissy with me, it made me feel very uncomfortable.

That being said, imagine the scene of two young kids sitting side by side, the girl leaning over to try to kiss a boy with a red face from embarrassment, his hands out the window, and the beginnings of an ulcer forming from all the sixth-grade-relationship stress.

One day, I was riding home with Regina and something in me snapped. I couldn't take the pressure anymore and was willing to do whatever I could to keep this girl from trying to make out with me. Enough was enough, and I needed a distraction. Without giving the situation much thought, I took the gum out of my mouth in preparation to throw it to the front of the bus. I don't know why the hell I came up with this idea, but I guess maybe self-consciously, the fight it would probably cause—chancing a possible accident—was better than just sitting in my seat with my sweaty hands and stomach pains. The gum however didn't quite make it to the front of the bus and, instead, bounced off the seat directly in front of Regina and me and landed in her hair. You can probably imagine my surprise when the gum didn't reach its intended destination. Of course, Regina's reaction to the slight navigational error was a little more surprising than my own.

I immediately apologized and tried to help take the gum out of her nappy mop, but at that time in my young life I didn't understand the science behind ripping a sticky substance out of human hair, so after screams only heard in horror movies, I stopped assisting Regina in the bubblegum–hair-removal process. I felt horrible for what had happened, but what was I supposed to do? Luckily enough, the stop I got off on came up shortly after that, and I wished her the best of luck as I made my way off the bus. She didn't thank me for my condolences for the loss of her hair, and I remember stepping off the bus thinking that was kind of rude of her.

I didn't sleep that well that night, because I kept going over in my head what had taken place on the bus that day. My mind raced from one thought to the next covering everything from bubblegum to world politics. I just lay there, and it seemed like I couldn't turn my brain off. I didn't think that was completely normal, but I didn't know well enough to ask anyone if they also lay in bed at night unable to fall asleep because of racing thoughts. Yet another sign that I probably should have spoken to someone about that.

The next day, I walked onto the bus and saw Regina sitting there with a considerable amount of hair missing from her head. If you ask me, no one deserves that, but she didn't really have "model" hair, so it's not like the world lost anything of significant value. The pope was still alive, so really, what are a few hairs, right? As I walked closer to "our" seat, she had an interesting look on her face that I couldn't quite place. It was a look that I had never seen before. I couldn't read it, and as I sat down I felt a very awkward tension between the two of us.

We sat there for quite a few minutes not saying a word to one another, and I knew I'd have to speak up. I had to be the bigger person and just tell her how sorry I was for what I'd done and that it wasn't intentional. Just when I opened my mouth to try to save our relationship, she smacked me right on the side of the head.

As expected by anyone in that situation, I reached up, grabbed my head, and yelled, "What the hell?" and it was only then that I felt a gigantic piece of juicy bubblegum stuck to my hair. She had planned the whole damn thing.

I'm not going to waste time going on and on about the process I went through to get the gum out of my hair, because that's not really important. What I learned that day was that girls are not the innocent, pink-dress, Barbie doll–playing, sweet people they make themselves out to be. They are vindictive, conspiring demons who will stop at nothing to make any poor defenseless boy's life a living hell. Needless to say ,Regina and I decided that it was probably mutually beneficial if we ended the life that we had built up until that point and went our separate ways. My first middle school relationship had ended, and the only thing I had to show for it was a new-found set of trust issues and a freshly made bald spot.

27

BLACKMAIL IS BETTER THAN NO MAIL

I learned very quickly that relationships in middle school were similar to those in elementary school—in terms of shelf life. The only difference was that snacks like cookies and candy were an acceptable sign of affection when you're younger, but when you get to middle school, the kids were giving each other jewelry. Well, at least in my school. You could look around the hall and see a boy and a girl walking together both wearing matching necklaces and shit. Okay, I can admit, it was kind of corny, but that's how we rolled.

With my relationship with Regina in the past, I decided to get right back on the horse and do what any kid in my position was expected to do: I needed to ask out her best friend. I mean, did you expect anything less from me?

Her name was Krissy Ivanhoe and she was a rather tall drink of water. I had never liked that in a girl when I was younger, because I didn't feel that girls should be tall. They were supposed to short and cute, not Amazonian and scary. In this case, I didn't have much choice in the matter, because Regina only had one best friend, so this was the card that I was dealt. I was going to play the shit out of it.

When I presented the question to Krissy, she naturally jumped at the idea of becoming my girlfriend, and it made me start to doubt the loyalty between female friends. It seemed that they were really close with one another until a guy came into the fold and then bye-bye girlfriend, hello boyfriend. I'm not complaining or anything, but at the same time, it's interesting to see how young a girl is when all that drama starts.

The only thing that was bad about Krissy, aside from her abnormal height and boring, straight hair, was the fact that she was a gift giver. She had a sterling silver necklace that she gave on loan to the guy she was with and would take great pride in repossessing it as soon as the relationship ended. At this time, it was my turn to wear the necklace, but I didn't have anything to give her in return. I saw the disappointment on her face when I had to deliver the news of my depressing financial situation. It was embarrassing, so to alleviate that feeling, I promised her that I would be getting her something very special soon.

Kids are inundated at a fairly young age with the idea that money doesn't grow on trees—in hopes of teaching them the value of money. I understood that value immediately because I knew that money was needed to buy what you wanted and needed, and what I wanted and needed was a gift to get Krissy off my back. But I had no money. So what does a stupid kid do in my position? Well, he goes out and steals it. Obviously. I've never been proud of the mistakes I've made in my life, and I promise you, this is no exception. When I got home that day, I went and took money out of my mother's purse, and after school the following day, I went and bought Krissy a ring.

There were two things wrong with this plan right out of the gate. One, when a woman has a bunch of kids, she knows how much money is in her purse; and two, of those many children, one of them was sure to find out and tattletale on you. Of course, in this case, that tattletale went by the name of big brother Jamie. He somehow received intel that his brother *may* have purchased a ring for some girl whom he was now with.

119

Now, typically a big brother would confront his little brother, find out he stole the money, and then tell on him, but oh no, not my brother. There was no profit in that plan, so why would he do that? Jamie knew that I stole the money, because that's the only way I could have gotten it, so he didn't even question me about that. Instead, he focused his talent on explaining to me that I would be his own personal slave for an undisclosed amount of time or he would leak the information of the stolen money to the parental authorities.

I had no choice but to go along with this plan, so I did the best I could in doing anything and everything my brother's demonic heart desired. The strain from the daily dose of blackmail, along with the fact that Krissy was rather pushy, overly affectionate, and a foot taller than the average height of a girl in her age group, sent me over the edge, and the relationship took a sudden turn down a street I was growing all-too familiar with, called I-Hate-You Road.

As if that wasn't bad enough, the blackmail continued until one day the shit hit the fan. My mother and stepfather called a meeting, and we all sat there in front of them and listened as they let us know that someone amongst us had illegally eaten a can of frosting that my mother had planned on using. This was one of only a few times I remember living in that house that something was missing and I wasn't the one who took it. I remember sitting there with a new feeling coming over me. I knew I was innocent, but after all the things I had taken over the years, I felt guilty about this latest crime. Unfortunately for me, those feelings never went away.

As the group interrogation continued, and no one was willing to confess to the cake frosting robbery of 1992, we were all sent to our rooms to deliberate until the criminal was brought to justice. One thing I can tell you about my big brother is that he had the patience of an ornery alligator. When Jamie wanted something done, he commanded our attention by either threatening us into doing it or somehow convincing us another way. Both of his methods were immoral at best, but each highly effective—how can you argue with that?

After what seemed to be at least an hour of deliberation, my brother grew tired and impatient and pulled me into a different room. He asked me, "Do you remember the time that you stole money from our mother to buy some girl a ring?"

I said, "Yeah, of course I remember, I've been your slave ever since."

He smiled as he looked down at me and said, "Well then, you're going to go downstairs and tell them that you ate the frosting, or I'm going down there and telling them that you stole the money."

Panic sunk in as my mind started to spin. He was an awful person for doing that to me, but I knew that he had me, and there was nothing I could do about it.

I walked downstairs with my head down, and as I walked through the living room and right up to the couch my parents were sitting on, I said the four words that to this day hurt my heart when I think about it. I said, "I ate the frosting."

My parents nodded as if they'd always assumed I was the one who did it anyways. I stood there ready to accept my punishment until my stepfather asked me a question that still baffles me. He asked, "Okay, Jason, how did you do it?"

I stood there kind of taken back and quickly wracked my brain searching for an answer. I said, "Well … I went downstairs one day and went into the pantry, grabbed the frosting, and opened it. Then I peeled back the metal top to it."

I couldn't believe that I was smart enough to remember that frosting had that sealed top to it, and I stood there kind of proud of myself. As odd as it may sound, I was getting away with coming up with a fake story, confessing to a crime that I didn't commit. Call it what you want, but I was feeling pretty good about myself.

The next question hit me so hard; I thought I was going to fall over. My stepfather asked, "Okay, okay, what flavor was it?" Guessing, I said, "Vanilla." His face changed immediately as he turned his head to look at my mother. He told me that would be enough and I was to return to my room.

I walked up those stairs and was greeted by Satan, and my brother asked me how it went. I told him that I thought it went okay and that I admitted to it. He asked me what my punishment was, and before I could tell him that I didn't get one yet, we heard my stepfather yell up the stairs for us all to come down.

Obeying his direction, we all marched downstairs, and once again sat in front of our parents. My stepfather spoke first as he explained how saddened they were that Jason had admitted to doing something that he really didn't do. My brother whipped his head over to me; the look in eyes could have killed a family of elves.

My stepfather continued the grand inquisition by asking the question all inquiring minds wanted to know. He looked at Jamie and said, "Now why would Jason admit to something he didn't do?"

Jamie said, "How do you know he didn't do it?"

John said, "Because the frosting was chocolate and Jason said he ate vanilla."

Jamie's face turned red, and he knew they knew he was responsible for my omission. What happened next turned my stomach so hard I thought I was going to be sick. Jamie confessed! He didn't say he ate the frosting, but he was nice enough to admit to forcing me to take the blame and then realizing he wasn't going down alone, he told them that I stole money from his mother.

I was shocked! How could he do that? After all the shit he'd put me through, how could it end like that? Naturally, no one gave a shit about some missing frosting when this new crime came into view. Jamie was off the hook. The real frosting thief was never caught, and I was now being brought up on charges of grand theft. Like many sentences, I don't remember what my punishment was because I had so many, but I'm sure it had something to do with not being allowed to date until marriage. Damn you, Jamie, and your big-brother right to torture every sibling younger than you!

28

HONORABLE MENTION

Being honorable has many different definitions. People form their own opinion about what honor looks like. In my life, two defining honorable moments really stand out, and both happened during my sixth-grade year. This is as good a time as any to mention them.

The first came during that highly transitional year. After two frustrating, failed relationships, I actually started to really focus on my studies, and when our report cards became available, I received a certificate stating that I had made something called the *honor roll*. Elementary school didn't have anything like that, so I wasn't sure what it really meant. I learned later on that it was a symbol of hard work in the field of academics.

I didn't possess the same amount of excitement as the other kids who had received one of these certificates. I didn't really care, and it showed. My mother, on the other hand, was very proud of my achievement, and that in itself changed my view on this whole honor-roll thing. I remember an instant feeling of self-gratification knowing that my mother was proud of me. I wanted to do it again and promised myself to never let go of the feeling I had when my mother was pleased with me. Unfortunately for me, self-sabotage was a gift I always kept giving myself, and that honor-roll certificate that sixth-grade year was the first and last time I would legitimately earn one.

The second honorable thing that I witnessed that year, oddly enough, came from my older brother, Jamie. I know what you're thinking, and trust me, I was surprised too, but this book is about sharing my life with you, and what he did has always captured a piece of my heart that, no matter what, he'll always have.

One day, Mama Darling was scheduled to come visit us, and needless to say, her visits brought excitement around our house only comparable to Christmas. Obviously, we were excited about seeing our grandmother, but let's be honest here, she spoiled the hell out of us, and that's what we were mostly excited about. We *loved* it. Nothing was too good for her grandkids, and she proved that to be her opinion every chance she got.

Sitting through class the day of her arrival would be very challenging for any kid knowing a person like her was going to be there when he got home, but for me it was even *more* challenging, because I had a hard time focusing as it was, let alone when something great was going to happen. That day was particularly tough for me, because I had done something wrong, and I was to stay after school for detention so, unlike the other kids, I would have to wait even longer to see Darling.

There was nothing I could do about it, but wait. As school ended and detention began, I started to experience something that I'm sure would be defined today as anxiety. I didn't want to be in that classroom staring at the board, paying for a crime I probably *did* commit, but at a cost I didn't agree with. Detention to me was retarded. I had to sit at a desk and only do my homework without saying a word to anyone else in the classroom. I rarely *ever* did my homework, so this was a really good opportunity for me. Come to think about it, I would guess that the only reason I made the honor roll was because the school was detaining me so much that I was completing all of my assignments.

My mother had told me that when I got out of detention, I was to go to a payphone and call her up so she would know when to come get me. That phone call was one that I was most excited to make. I couldn't wait for detention to end so I could run across the street, make the call, and be one step closer to seeing Darling.

When the detention warden released us from educational prison, I bolted out of that room like my ass cheeks were on fire. I don't remember a time I ever ran that fast. When I arrived at the payphone, there were two girls standing there, and one of them was yapping away to someone on the other line about something to do with hairspray and tight, rolled jeans. They were laughing with their stupid laughs, and I started to feel a tightness building in my chest. All I wanted to do was call home, so my mother could come pick me up.

I stood there, sweat starting to form on my upper lip, my hands starting to shake. I reached into my pocket and grabbed the dime that I would use to call home with.[4] I started to pace back and forth and the motor mouth's girlfriend noticed my impatient pacing and gave me a look as if to say, "Um yeah, our lives are more important than yours, so wait your turn."

Of course, I didn't appreciate that look, so I said to her, "Can you please tell your friend that I need to use the phone?"

Without hesitation, the girl talking and talking on the phone stopped talking, put the phone over her shoulder, and said to me, what I had never heard anyone say before. She said, "I'll get off the phone when pigs fly out of my butt."

I stood there *shocked* at what I'd just heard. What did that mean? Was she serious about that? I knew that I was an honor-roll student now and expected to be highly intelligent, but was I really going to have to wait to call home until a pig actually flew out of her ass? I wasn't sure what to do at that point, so I said the only thing I could say. I replied with, "Well, it looks like that already happened," and then I pointed to her equally ugly friend standing next to her. That of course wasn't the nicest things to say. But they had made me very angry with the threat of never being able to use the phone, let alone something disgusting to do with swine.

I don't think motor mouth's friend liked my comment, because she pointed at me with a finger that wasn't her pointer finger. Then

[4] Yeah, I said it; phone calls back then were ten cents!

in an attempt to defend her girlfriend from the likes of me, the girl on the phone said, "Now, we're never going to let you use this phone. We'll be here all night if we need to."

At that point, I had just about had it and decided to make a decision that seemed to me, at the time, to be the most sound in judgment. I went right up to the girl on the phone, and slowly pushed down the little metal lever, disconnecting her phone call, and then turned around and pointed to her friend with the same finger she pointed at me with. Naturally, they didn't like that, and before I knew it, they were storming away yelling at me about how they were going to tell their boyfriends on me.

I said okay and waved to them as I turned toward the phone and finally got to make my call.

I got home and got to see Darling. Was there a better way to end a day? That night, I didn't give those stupid girls any real thought, but let my mind drift off to a peaceful place as I fell asleep with ease for what was one of the very few times in recent memory.

The next day at school wasn't as peaceful as my great night of sleep, as I got off the bus and was met by the two biggest eighth-graders ever created. Their names were Brutus and Bubba. I wouldn't be exaggerating when I say that their parents had to be shooting steroids the night they procreated these kids. They were gigantic!

In middle school, fights usually start by a lot of talking back and forth from one side to the next by giving examples of what each person is going to do. This case was no different. Those two knuckleheads stood in front of me and explained in great detail about how they were going to rip off my legs and kick my ass with them. I actually remember laughing in their faces, not because I was a tough guy, but more because I had instantly gotten an image of that beating and it was kind of funny. Unfortunately, they didn't find it as funny as I did, and just when one of them reached back to strike me, a couple teachers came running in and grabbed them.

As they were being dragged off to the principal's office, the boyfriend to the girl I'd hung up the phone on yelled out that he was going to kill me. I of course didn't help the situation when I yelled back, "Are you going to use my own legs for that or should we borrow someone else's?" My ability to be a smartass is self-proclaimed as legendary.

The reality of this death threat didn't really kick in till later that day, and by the time I got home, I was sick to my stomach at the thought of dying soon. I didn't want to die. Darling was here, and when she came to visit, the amount of groceries we had in the house was unprecedented. I couldn't die now, not with all this food here! I had the worst sleep that night that I'd ever had as I lay there thinking about who would attend my funeral and what would they say. I mentally ran down the list of what some of my family would say:

My mother: "Well, at least he made the honor roll once."

My stepfather: "I'm going to have to punish *someone* for this."

Jamie: "Hmmm, does this mean, *I'm* going to have to shovel all the snow myself?"

Dani: "Should I confess to eating the frosting now or ..."

Before I knew it, I was waking up with a big smile on my face, and it stayed there until I remembered that I was probably going to die that day. I was hoping for snow or something to cancel school, but no such luck. It was seventy degrees with clear skies and a chance for death.

When I got off the bus, I started to walk really fast to my classroom, and as I neared the building and hope started to build in my chest that I was going to be safe, I felt someone grab my arm. I spun around ready to start punching anything, when I noticed that one of my sixth-grade teachers, Mr. Totleman was standing there. I told him that I needed to get inside.

He said, "Calm down Jason, you don't have to run, I want to show you something." He walked me over to a large group of people. We walked through the crowd, and in the middle of the group stood two really tall eighth-graders. At first I didn't know what the hell was going on. Did Mr. Totleman set this whole thing up? Was he TRYING to see me get my ass kicked? I stood there as the larger of the two boys came up to me, and I prepared for my beating. I covered my head and waited.

After a couple of seconds of nothingness, I opened my eyes, and there in front of me was an outstretched hand. It belonged to Brutus. I hesitantly shook it as he whispered the words I *never* expected to hear. He said, "I'm sorry about everything." And with that, he walked away.

I couldn't believe what had just happened. My brother Jamie never said a word to me about it, but I found out through the grapevine that Jamie *somehow* found out that a couple of kids were going to kill his brother, and then *somehow* found Brutus's number and called him up. The details I got were that Jamie said to leave me alone and Brutus told him that I had hung up the phone on his girlfriend. What Jamie said next single-handedly changed the way I viewed him growing up. He said, "I don't care if Jason pissed in your mouth, if you hurt him, I will end your life."

With that, Brutus apologized to me in front of the whole school, including Mr. Totleman. My relationship with Jamie has always been rocky, but that show of care and support is something that I will never forget.

29

LAST CALL

The rest of sixth grade proved to be slightly uneventful. I tried harder and harder to get on the honor roll again, but my grades got worse and worse. I did pass, but the honor roll eluded me, and I couldn't do anything about it.

As the year neared the end, the school put on a dance for the sixth-grade students. I had gotten in trouble for something I did at some point, and though I can't remember what it was that I did wrong, I *do* remember that my parents' punishment for it was to not be able to attend the dance. That punishment was another one I would choose to ignore. Besides, it was a dance! And I enjoyed dancing. I'm not sure in what world my parents actually thought I wouldn't attend it. Some parents are a little on the nutty side—a side that most children will just never understand ... until we have kids.

Knowing that I would be at that dance at the end of the day, I started to get ready for it in the morning before school. I couldn't get too ready, because after all, I didn't want anyone thinking I was going, so I rushed out the door not as "done up" as I would have liked to be.

After school that day, the kids attending the dance went to the cafeteria where the sweet sounds of C+C Music Factory and Boyz

II Men were pumping. I can't tell you that I had the time of my life at that dance, because in the back of my mind I knew that I would need to somehow get home and face the firing squad for my latest crime, but all things considered, I still had a pretty decent time.

After a couple hours of pounding down the punch, I needed to use the bathroom, and during my time in the tiny sixth-grade urinal, I noticed that in rushing to get ready this morning, I hadn't remembered to apply deodorant. I was not happy about that situation! But then, the dance was ending soon and I didn't have a date, so it didn't matter too much. To play it safe, I decided to leave a little early. As I started to say goodbye to my friends, a girl came up to me and said that Kerry (the girl of my first kiss, years ago) was moving out of state and she wanted to dance with me before she left.

I felt really sad as I told her that I couldn't dance with Kerry. I didn't want to turn down the offer—because after all, she was my first kiss—but my arm pits were stinky, and I couldn't bear the thought of that embarrassment. I watched as the girl walked over to Kerry and delivered the news. I turned my back and walked away immediately after I noticed that tears were forming in Kerry's eyes. If only I was "allowed" to attend the dance! I wouldn't have rushed that morning, and I could have properly said goodbye to her. As dumb as it sounds, I've never forgotten that, and to this day, still feel bad about it.

That situation officially ended the sixth grade, and after finding out that my grades were just good enough to send me to the seventh grade, I prepared myself for a summer away from middle school, away from my parents, and most importantly, away from any sense of depressive reality.

30

THE START OF SOMETHING NOT SO SPECIAL

Ah, seventh grade. This year was as enjoyable to me as the prospect of a Mexican hangover. The classes were much harder in seventh grade than they were in sixth grade, and I'd had a hard enough time with those—so imagine how happy I was with these?

I had a lot of teachers that year, and just as the year before, they were hardly significant enough to mention, with the exception of one. What his name really was doesn't matter, but it sounded like fellatio, and I can tell you that it was one name that my classmates and I would whisper with confidence behind his back as soon as we realized what a dickhead he was. So for the sake of the story, we'll just call him, Mr. Head. Since he was both my seventh-grade science and homeroom teacher, I was fortunate enough to get Head twice a day.

Seventh-grade science was a lot different from what I was used to. Typically, school was all about memorization. With the exception of math, the only time you really utilized what you learned was when you took tests. Other than that, school had been a complete waste of time. This year would be the first one you really had to apply what you were learning. Like dissecting a frog for example—who the hell thought of that idea?

No, seriously, I want to know, so I can personally thank him or her for ruining my childhood attraction to Kermit. Have you ever had to dissect a frog before? It's fucked up to say the least, and I don't care how much you tell me they don't feel a thing. After having to dissect a frog, I can't even watch the Muppets without wanting to cry.

I had a huge problem with this activity and very clearly expressed my concerns to Mr. Head. His response was something along the lines of, "Okay, then I guess you want an F in this class, correct?"

Yeah, asshole, that's what I've always dreamed of, a failing grade. That was the first altercation I had with this guy and certainly not the last.

Another problem with Mr. Head was that he had a Short Man Complex. He always used to stick out his tiny, round chest when he walked as if he were king of the roost. I did not like that at all. I wasn't sure why it made me so uncomfortable that, sitting there, I had to shoot him the stinky retinas, but I didn't care about the reason; he was getting them no matter what.

Mr. Head also had an attraction to faded blue Dockers and wore them daily as if they were a required piece of clothing. I know it may sound like I'm nitpicking here, but think about it: how can you know a bunch of things regarding science, but still can't figure out how to wash your clothes without taking the color out of them? This guy was a phony, and I saw right through him *and* his outdated Dockers.

31

A Mistake Followed by a Great Loss

W e all do things in our lives that we look back on and wish we hadn't done. That feeling is known as regret. I've never met someone who has never experienced regret before. I myself, experience regret on a daily basis. When you're supposed to be bipolar, the racing thoughts are enough to drive you more insane than you're already clinically considered. One of the things I think about a lot that I wish I could take back was something I erased my seventh-grade year.

My grandfather *and* godfather, Papa Dan (my father's father), was an extraordinary man. I hear stories about him even to this day that make me smile. He was a boxer, an inventor, and a hard worker just to name a few qualities. But those didn't mean a thing, because more importantly, he was a family man's man. We can all talk about how close we are to our families, but can you ask yourself if you've displayed a lifetime of togetherness and come up with the answer "Yes?" I know I can't, but the most important stories I got that pertained to Papa Dan were the descriptions of him being a person who not only held his family together, but also taught that family how to stay together long after he was gone.

Papa Dan was also a bit of an entertainer and loved when his family got together on Sundays. I witnessed this weekly ritual a lot in my younger years and remember loving every minute of it. On occasion, Papa Dan would sing a song about Peter Pan, and I was fortunate enough to have recorded it onto a mini tape. Whenever I had the chance to play the tape I would, because it gave me a clear picture of him sitting in his chair at the dining room table singing it to everyone. It was always standing room only, and we always loved hearing it.

The first true lesson about life I learned came that seventh-grade year. Up until that point, I was innocent in my knowledge about life and how precious it is. I unknowingly took advantage of it the day I taped over Papa Dan's performance. And just because I was showing off the mini tape recorder he had given me in class. Of course, when I realized I had taped over the song, I just assumed that I would be able to get a new recording soon. Life has a shitty way of showing you that you don't know anything about anything.

Papa Dan had gotten cancer and fought it very hard. My father would go on for years talking about something known as the "Ventre Strength," and Papa Dan was no exception to that. But life hits harder than the people living it are, and I remember finding out that Papa Dan was sent home from the hospital one day to spend his remaining time with his family. We all carry around a selfish bone somewhere in our bodies, but Papa Dan accepting his fate and deciding that family meant more to him than trying to get more time for himself opened my eyes and made me learn that there are some people out there that aren't selfish. Of all the things I remember about him, including the things I only heard about him, his acceptance over denial is what I admire the most.

My father picked us up that weekend like he had almost every weekend for as long as I could remember. That weekend, however, was not one that I can put on the books as an enjoyable time. We were driven to Papa Dan and Mama Rose's condo, and when I walked in, I saw Papa Dan in his hospital bed in the living room. He had been losing weight for quite some time, but how he looked that day was not the man I'd grown up admiring. It couldn't have been. He was there physically, and you could tell that it was a fight for him just to smile, but I remember looking down on him and feeling how hard it was to witness what he was going through. How selfish was that? He was dying right in front of us, and I had a hard time watching it!

Next to the bed was a chair, and I spent a lot of that day in it, just holding his hand. There wasn't a lot of strength in it, but what I felt was the closeness he showed me every time I saw him. I remember sitting there next to him thinking about the science papers he'd helped me out with, and the poker games during which I sat next to him. The family get-togethers and slumber parties my siblings and I had all snuggled up in sleeping bags right below his bed. I remembered all the times I stood outside with him and watched him smoke his cigars, the smoke slowly disappearing into the sky and the enjoyment he received from them. I hated sitting next to Papa Dan that day, but I sat there anyways, and those last few minutes with him is a memory that I will always hold dear to my heart. It's a memory that, without his strength, I wouldn't have had.

When we left his house that day and my father drove us home, it wasn't very long till we learned that Papa Dan stopped fighting and drifted off. My mother told us that if we didn't want to go to school the next day, she understood, but I went anyways. The funeral was set. It would be the first one that I would remember attending. The service itself was as beautiful as any service could be, I guess. There was a large turnout of people who loved and respected him. I guess that's all we can ask for: to live a life in which there are all good things said about us when we're gone. In that category, Papa Dan was more than a winner.

When we all went over to the church, I sat there and watched as my father and uncles stood up to speak. Up to that point, my father and his brothers were not people I ever saw get emotional like that. Time spent with them was always time spent laughing. No tears. This time was different, and as I sat there that day, I felt a pain that I had never experienced before. I had spent a lifetime showing people how hurt they made me feel, but that day was the first day in my young life that I felt *real* pain. Not pain predicated on the constant desire to win achievement by pretending to feel it. This was real. This was horrible.

When the people who had decided to say a few words had finished, the priest quietly asked if anyone else would like to say something. My mind wanted to jump out of that chair and yell, "Me! I do!". To let it be known not just by his kids but also by one of his grandkids that he was a great man. I wanted to run up to that podium as fast I could, but the pain I felt planted me in that pew, and I was unable to move. I was frozen by hurt, doubt, and fear. I was paralyzed by the inability to act. I was a coward.

After the service ended, we went over to the burial site to end a funeral that should never have been taking place. I stood there that day ashamed of myself for not being able to speak on behalf of myself, my siblings and my cousins. I remember the promise I made to myself that day that if, God forbid, I was ever in a position to publicly speak about a lost loved one, I would take advantage of that. I would not succumb to fear. I would not just sit there and bottle up everything I was feeling. That promise is one that I held close to my chest for around sixteen years. It was a promise I made to myself that I would learn was a promise I couldn't keep.

32

FIGHTING TO MOVE

Sometime after the devastation my family and I went through from the death of Papa Dan, the time to move into a new school had arrived, and the students and faculty were running around like Christmas elves just days before December 25. It was pandemonium. One would think that they'd hire a bunch of movers and get everything done over Christmas break or wait till the summer, but that would make too much sense. Instead, the school board decided to make the move during normal school hours. The distraction in itself was epic. Each classroom was stacked high with books and furniture and everything else you can think of in order to make the move possible. Just having to deal with that distraction was enough to warrant giving each kid an honorary passing grade, but my luck was as good back then as it is now, and a passing grade was the furthest thing being offered to the students.

When we got to our new school however, I can honestly say that the building was beautiful. They spared no expense in building a school that was long overdue. The halls were large, the classrooms larger, and everyone around me seemed very excited to start their new life in a building that promised to produce the brightest minds of our generation. Even I was excited about it and hopped on the bandwagon thinking that a new school was the only thing standing in my way to reaching academic greatness.

Like all new things, the feeling of something fresh withered away too soon, however, and I was right back where I left off. I was in school, I didn't like it, and I wanted out. With each new day, I grew more tired of the daily grind. I couldn't place what was happening to me, but I grew less and less patient with people, and instead of just acting out in class for a couple of laughs, I was getting into arguments with other kids. And once I got angry, I had a really hard time calming down. I look back on it now and realize how significant that change was in me—*it was not normal.* But it was all I knew, so I was not sure it wasn't normal. I wish that I'd known enough to ask for help, but when you're going through it, the last thing you want to admit to is being abnormal.

One day during English class, I got in an argument with some kid by the name of Reece. He was a short, black kid, heavier than I was, and definitely meaner. I was confident that if push came to shove, I would lose that fight, and I think that was probably the reason I egged it on. I didn't want to give anyone the impression that I could lose. As the argument grew louder, our teacher got involved. She decided I was the aggressor and sent me to the principal's office. On the way there, some kid passed me in the hallway and accidentally brushed my shoulder. That was enough to set me off; so I pushed him. He pushed me back, and then I punched him in the face. We rolled around the hallway like a couple of drunk teletubbies until someone broke us apart and dragged us to the principal's office. I didn't care though, because after all, I was heading there anyways.

I was looking at a possible suspension for assaulting this poor kid, and my parents were notified. There were so many things going through my mind at that time, so being sent home for an extended amount of time was an option that I welcomed. I didn't care what punishment my parents were going to give me, so long as I wouldn't have to be in that school at that time.

I had friends over the years who had gotten suspended, and part of me envied their situation, because people always liked the person associated with a suspension story. I wanted to be one of them. However, my luck being similar to a gambler who can't win ended up granting me a day's suspension *in* school instead of out of school. That is hands down the worst thing you can give to a kid. They stick you in a room with a desk and make you do homework all day. The psychology behind the punishment was genius, because chances were, if you got suspended for something, you probably don't hold school itself in high regard, so homework is probably the last thing you would complete on a daily basis. Having to do homework for eight hours straight is like forcing a vegan to partake in a hot dog eating contest. It's pure madness. What made this punishment even *worse* than the aforementioned was that the poor kid who I assaulted for no reason got suspended as well and had to sit in the chair right next to me all day. I felt like such an asshole.

At first glance, I would say that the punishment worked in teaching me not to act like such a prick in school, because I promised myself to *never* get in trouble again. There was no way that I could sit through another day of purgatory. It was boring! It was unpleasant, and quite frankly, it made me angry. How odd is that? I clearly had anger issues already—getting in a fight for no good reason?—so they stick me in a room that makes me angrier than I was before I stepped foot in it. Nice. I felt confident about keeping my promise to stay out of trouble. Of course, me being me, I would break that promise mere weeks after making it.

33

HE TOOTH FAIRY IS A GUY

School wasn't getting any easier, to say the least, and I found myself looking for any excuse I could come up with to get out of it. Unfortunately, when your mother is a nurse, the traditional methods of faking an illness are not going to work. I remember witnessing my brother doing the old "thermometer by the heater" trick and then watching as my mother looked at him as if to say, "Jamie, I know you don't have a 115-degree temperature, get your things, you're going to school." She was very quick, and just had a way of ensuring that her children were going to go and get an education no matter what.

There was no way around her. If you complained of a headache, you got aspirin; if you went further by claiming you might have strep throat, she performed a throat culture. I believe that my unrelenting ability to come up with creative ways to get out of things was because of her unrelenting ability to find ways to stop me. Needless to say, I had a lot of practice growing up.

Sitting in Mr. Head's class one day, I decided it was time to go home and it had been a while since anyone had pulled the old "I Just Threw Up" routine. School nurses for the most part were very thorough in their examinations, but when it came to vomit, forget about it. They avoided you like the plague. My mother, on the other hand, welcomed involuntary stomach convulsions as if they were a tax credit. There was no fooling her. I think that when a mother gives birth, she develops a sixth, seventh, eighth, and Spidey sense that alerts her to when her children are full of shit. It was a school policy to send children home if they threw up in school, but I don't know what my mother said to that nurse, because a few minutes into the phone call, my pretend sickness was somehow cured, and I was being sent back to class.

Going back into Mr. Head's class gave me the feeling similar to what I would learn later in life to be called the *walk of shame*. It was just downright embarrassing. Then it made me very angry to be embarrassed, and I couldn't just let this stand. I needed to come up with a way to get back at my mother for her refusal to save me from a day in the life of the seventh-grade student. I would show her.

Mr. Head at that point was going on and on about something to do with whatever it was I wasn't paying attention to, and to get my mind off of his annoying voice, I decided to pay attention to the last remaining baby tooth I had in my mouth. I can't say that the tooth was loose, but after a few minutes of screwing with it, I made it loose. As the world of science dragged on and on, I loosened that tooth more and more. Eventually, with a quick twist and a pull, the tooth popped out into my hand along with quite a bit of blood. It would have been easy for me to just excuse myself to the bathroom, clean up, and then head back to the nurse's office, but what kind of Jason Ventre would I be if I didn't cause some sort of scene? After letting a good amount of blood drip into my hands, I held the bloody digits up into the air and yelled that my teeth were falling out. With that, I was sent to the nurse's office.

I sat there smiling with my remaining teeth, knowing that I was going home for sure this time. Think about it: I was supposedly vomiting AND NOW I *was* losing my teeth ... There was no way they would keep me in school. How could they? I HAD to have some disease. Looking up at a nurse who was trying to stay as far

141

away from me as she could, I watched as she once again picked up the phone and called my mother.

I imagined the fear Nurse Needle would hear in my mother's voice as she would race to the school, pick me up in her arms, and drive a hundred miles an hour to the hospital, praying that her son would make it. I was sure I would be rushed right into Intensive Care, all eyes on me as the doctors did everything they could to save my life. Of course, I would survive and wake up in the recovery room with my mother sitting right next to my bed, holding my hand, and crying from sheer joy that her little boy was alive. I continued smiling as I pictured the doctor coming in to deliver the news to my mother. She would immediately stand up, her hands shaking as the doctor looked her in the eyes and said, "Ma'am, you're son doesn't need glasses, now go back to class ..."

I immediately snapped out of my daydream when Nurse Needle repeated herself, saying, "Jason, your mother says you're fine. Now go back to class." I couldn't freakin' believe it! For all my mother knew, I was throwing up, bleeding, and my teeth were falling out of my face, and I STILL had to stay in school. I once again had to take the walk of shame back through Mr. Head's science class.

He smugly smiled at me as if to say, "Back already? I knew you were full of shit." When I sat back down in my seat, I stared back at him wanting to jump over the table and attack him for being such a dick. A few minutes later, Mr. Head must've gotten tired of me giving him the stinky retinas, because he walked over to me, leaned over the table, and placed a quarter in front of me. He said, "That's for the tooth," and walked away. To this day, I *still* have a deep-seated hatred for the tooth fairy.

34

PROCRAST-INVENTION

Seventh grade carried on at its usual pace, comparable to a retarded snail. Life just couldn't move fast enough for me, and I remember that always being a problem. I sat in class most days wondering why the second hand on the clock moved so slow and then further wondered why I was stuck in the seat I was sitting in. Letting my mind wander seemed to be the only thing I could do in school to let time go by faster. If they could come up with a class in which the idea would be for the student to slip into a daze, I surely would have been awarded a scholarship to some ivy league college before I even got to high school! Could you imagine? Me, Jason Ventre, the Doogie Howser of daydreaming. Hey, it could happen.

I sat there in class that day thinking about my latest irrelevant-to-life fantasy, and as a big smile formed, Mr. Head interrupted the happy thoughts with his own version of what could be constituted as fun. A Science Fair. Now, this wasn't any ordinary science fair—this was for inventors! This was serious stuff. Head walked around the room going over the seriousness of this fair. He explained that a majority of the grade in his class would be from the outcome of the invention we were to come up with and all the work associated with it. I guess he was grading heavily on this assignment, because it was going to take half the school year to finish.

But I didn't like the sound of this whole *Science Inventors Fair* right from the start. For one thing, I was never good at going home and doing homework, let alone going home and working on something day in and day out. Secondly, what was I going to invent? My imagination invented odd fantasies, but I was sure that I wouldn't be able to market those. I felt nervous, and I immediately wanted to leave class, to run away and be as far away as I could from this building and the homework assignments that were in it.

When I got home from school that day I remember sitting on the couch trying to come up with ideas on what I would invent. I wondered if I could get away with inventing a new school in which kids weren't pressured and confronted with the kind of constant anxiety I felt from all the homework assignments and testing. A school in which children were rewarded with positive reinforcement when he or she came up short from attempting to learn instead of faced with the threat of a bad grade or a phone call home to the parents. I understood, even at that young an age, the importance of structure, but at the same time, I couldn't help but disagree with the structure I had experienced.

Deciding at that point that inventing a new school wasn't going to fly, I came up with the next best idea. Why don't I just steal someone else's idea? That way, I don't have to stress about coming up with my own. Luckily enough for me, Papa Dan had come up with an idea to invent a device that made it easier to see traffic lights. Of course, Papa Dan didn't just stop at the idea; he built a mockup. I decided that since the project was already done and the invention was awesome, I was sure to pass seventh grade science without doing any work. My plan was genius. It was flawless. The assignment called for the creativity and discipline to come up with an invention, but I invented a plan in which I would use someone else's. This might sound very unethical, but when you're in seventh grade, you look for any way to educationally survive.

We had a week to come up with the idea, but since I already had an idea, I spent the week watching television and playing outside with my friends. When the day arrived for us to speak in class about our idea, I was excited. Papa Dan's invention was sure to turn some heads, and the best part about it was the fact that I didn't have to put any work into it. I had found a way to beat the system, and I clearly remember feeling pride about that. I was a thirteen-year- old kid who was happy he'd found a way to cheat.

When Mr. Head turned to me and asked me to stand up and let the class know of the invention I had come up with, I stood up ... but very slowly ... as if the ... time ... I was taking ... to stand ... was *my* time ... and ... my time ... was more valuable ... than anyone else's. I instantly became cocky and overconfident. I don't know why it was happening, but it was. When I finally finished the process of standing up, I looked around the room with a half-smile. After scanning the room with my smirk a few times, I stopped and let the grin rest in a pointed direction at Mr. Head. When I was ready, I spoke about Papa Dan's invention as if it were the second-coming of Christ. I felt that I confidently sold the idea so well that I started to imagine I was in the middle of a New York trade room in which everyone around me had order tickets begging me to sell, sell, sell. I was on top of the world again, and soon I would be rich!

My limitless fortune fantasy was cut a little prematurely when I heard Mr. Head open up his mouth and utter the words that to this day give me the angry bumps. He said, "I don't get it."

How could he not? I stood there wanting to explode. My heart was pounding at an abnormal rate, and I felt the fire building in my stomach. I was mad, but I had to try to find a way to control it. I started taking slow, deep breaths. When I felt my pulse start to slow, I re-explained the invention to Mr. Head, thinking that maybe in my overconfident haste, I hadn't explained it very well. This time, I spoke slower and more clearly, and when I was done, Mr. Head said, "Yeah, I got that, but I still don't get it."

Now I was just shocked. He clearly understood what the invention was all about; he was just being a dickhead about it for some reason. I bet it was because he was still annoyed about the time I interrupted his class to pull out my own tooth. Behind me, I heard a couple of kids snickering, and I immediately felt dumb and vulnerable.

I looked at Mr. Head and said, "Whatever" as I sat down.

He said, "What did you say?"

Now, feeling like I was being challenged, I slowly spoke, as if was speaking to a person hard of hearing, I said, "W-H-A-T-E-V-E-R."

Mr. Head was in no mood to be spoken to like that, so he said the line I heard so many teachers say to me when I displayed a lack of interest in their bullshit. He said, "So I guess you don't care about your grade then either. Maybe your parents would like to know about that."

I looked up at him, and the fire I felt in my stomach was moving farther and farther up my entire body. I could feel my face getting hot, and I was sure the color of it was a deep, deep red. I'd had enough of this guy. I'd had enough of people using the fear a young kid has of getting in trouble with his parents as an excuse for why they should conform to the wishes of a teacher who clearly didn't know the right way to communicate with the many different personalities that rested in the minds of the students he was paid to mold. I dramatically ripped a piece of paper out of my notebook and wrote seven tiny numbers on it. Then I got out of my chair, walked over to Mr. Head's desk, slapped the paper down in front of him, leaned over, and whispered the words sure to get me suspended.

I said, "If you want to talk to my parents, here's their number." I didn't care anymore, and I was determined to show him. Standing in front of him, we stared into each other's eyes for what seemed like an eternity. Then when I felt it was time, I turned around, walked slowly back to my seat, sat down, and stared at him until the bell rang.

I went through the rest of the day knowing that he was surely going to call my parents. Hell, I even gave him the number so he didn't have to look it up. When I got home from school, I walked in the door expecting World War III, but instead, it was just a normal day. Turns out, Mr. Head never called my parents. To this day, I'm not sure why he decided not to tell on me, but I remember having a shred of respect for that guy that day, despite what we had been through together that year.

35

AND THE WINNER IS ...

The next couple of months flew by without incident in science class. I continued to not do any of the work associated with the science project, because all I really had to do was show up with the physical invention the day of the fair with some display boards describing what it was.

It was a Friday afternoon when Mr. Head reminded the class that the Science Invention Fair was going to be on Tuesday, so we would have to have our inventions in class on Monday to submit them to the fair. That was perfect for me, because my father was picking us up on Saturday morning for our weekend visit, so all I had to do was somehow take Papa Dan's mockup home with me and let the rest of the pieces fall into place.

This weekend was no different than any other weekend. I was excited to see my father like I was excited to see him every weekend. It was always pretty much the same routine. We'd get there on Saturday morning and relax around the house a little or go play basketball or do whatever we wanted to. Then at lunchtime, my stepmother pulled out the lunchmeat. She was a tactician with the sandwiches and knew what each one of us kids liked on ours. I was a turkey-and-cheese kid all growing up—and still am the same way to this day. Jamie was a ham-and-cheese kid. I don't remember what my sisters were, but that's the point I'm trying to make. My stepmother saw us six days a month and knew what we *all* liked. I saw my siblings *every day* of the month, and I can only tell you what one of them liked. In that respect, she was an amazing woman, and I always have held a place in my heart for the interest she took in us kids regardless of the outcome.

After lunch on Saturdays, my father usually wanted to do something with us—like see a movie or something similar to that. Of course, we never complained because we all enjoyed getting spoiled. What kid wouldn't? After our Saturday activity, there was usually a really nice dinner that my stepmother cooked. Then after dinner, we would all watch a movie or television together. Sunday morning was a gourmet breakfast with eggs, bacon, sausage, pancakes, you name it, and our stepmother cooked that too. Then we went to church, and then it was time to watch football. After football, it was just a matter of lounging around the house eating and spending time together.

Throughout all these activities on this weekend, I tried to find a good time to ask my father for permission to take Papa Dan's invention home with me. I don't know why it was so hard to ask him. I'm sure subconsciously I had a hard time asking, because Papa Dan had passed away, but this was *my* father, and I was his son. It shouldn't have been that hard.

As time got closer for my father to take us home, I started to feel desperate and decided that I was going to have to just steal the mockup. I waited for the right moment to make my move, and when that moment presented itself, I ran downstairs to the basement, saw Papa Dan's invention sitting on his old drafting table and picked it up. I looked at it, my heart racing a mile a minute, and then placed it back down where I got it from. I couldn't do it. It didn't feel right. I had skated through months of science class because I knew that I didn't *have* to do the work, and now I would have to face the consequences for my actions.

The next day in class, Mr. Head asked me where my project was, and I held my head high as I told him that I didn't have it with me and would not have it tomorrow during the fair. He nodded and went on to look at the project of the kid next to me. I failed. A depressive state of mind came over me as I sat there thinking about the fact that I wasn't even a good thief. How could you do *that* wrong? I was going to have to repeat the seventh grade. I couldn't believe it.

As life shows us, sometimes on a daily basis, we don't know half of what we think we know. Mr. Head ended up giving me a very low grade in that class, but somehow he recommended that I get promoted to the eighth grade. Coincidentally enough, all my teachers recommended the same thing. I don't care if they passed me so they didn't have to be with me for another year, or that they felt that I did enough to get by. The fact of the matter was that I was moving on to eighth grade.

I sat in my chair on the last day of school rereading that report card as if someone had made a dire mistake. The shock I felt was abnormal. Someone was looking out for me, and I made a promise to myself that day. I promised that eighth grade was going to be different. I was going to try to put my conspiracy theories aside. I would actually make an effort to learn something. I would stop blaming others for my failures. Eighth grade would be the year that Jason Ventre turned his life around. Nothing was going to stop me, and it would the understatement of the year to say that I was looking forward to school next year.

PART 3

36

ARIZONA SUCKS

I was fourteen years old when my mother uprooted us to the great state of Arizona. She'd always wanted to live out there. I never wanted to. To this day, I still have a bad taste in my mouth for Arizona, and it stems back to that very first move so many years ago.

My mother's way of making this move possible was through my stepfather. As you know, he was a police officer, so my mother sold him on the idea of Arizona, and all he had to do was get accepted to the Tucson Police Academy. After a couple of years of flying back and forth, they received word that he'd passed all the tests, and a date was given for him to start the academy. I can't speak on behalf of the rest of my siblings, but the news was devastating to me. My whole family was on the East Coast, and I'm expected to just pack some things and leave them? That move is still one of the only things I hold against my mother that I don't think will ever go away.

Playing the devil's advocate, I could see that the high school my siblings and I would have ended up at in Torrington was not the best of schools, so if her reasoning was to better the educational possibilities for her children, then great, but in my heart, I just think she wanted to be in an area that offered her something that she'd always wanted—whatever that reason actually was.

37

THE TALK

I remember the talk like it was yesterday. My mother and stepfather sat Kellie, me, and Dani down to deliver the news. (Jamie at the time was already living with my father for reasons only he can tell you) There wasn't any excitement involved with the news. I'm sure my mother tried to build up the decision to take us there, but all I remember was the news delivered in the form of a threat. They told us that our father was probably going to tell us that if we want to stay in Connecticut with him and our stepmother, he would fight for us. I'm smiling inside as I'm writing this because, I knew without a doubt that he would fight for us. But, like any good feeling, it was short-lived and followed up with a guarantee that no matter what, regardless if we were of age to decide, there was nothing anyone could do: we would be moving to Tucson. It truly came across as a threat. As a young boy, I remember thinking that the decision was mine, but my mother and stepfather always had a way of sitting you down and explaining to you that you don't have a choice. There is no gray area. This is what is happening.

I learned later in life that there's a sales tactic called Bully Sales. It's a way of selling something by convincing your potential customer that not only do you have what they need, but because of certain situations, it would behoove them to buy from you. I felt sick to my stomach knowing that soon I would have to face my father and talk about this ridiculous idea of leaving him and everyone we knew for what seemed to me to be one woman's desperate attempt to seek her own version of happiness.

Like every Saturday morning, my father picked us up and took us back to his town of Prospect. There wasn't much time wasted when we got there. My father held a meeting upstairs with all of us; he said that he had heard the news and that if any of us—or perhaps all us—wanted to stay with him, he would fight for us until the end. He went around the room and asked each one of us what our decision was. I lost a piece of myself that day when I looked my father in his eyes and told him that I wanted to move to Arizona with my mother.

I look back on that day and feel ashamed for my decision. I caved-in to a threat and it wasn't even a good one. I saw the hurt and age in my father's eyes. Unfortunately, that won't be the last time that I'll be responsible for causing that.

I felt defeated. Why couldn't I have been man enough to say, "Fuck no. My whole family is here. Go off and get a sunburn, I'm staying here where people are honest, sincere, family-oriented, and know how to cook." Instead, I'd said, "Yes suh, massa" and then sang the lyrics to "Swing Low, Sweet Chariot."

That move to Tucson would start a chain of impulsive decisions that would eventually put me on a path consistently heading in the wrong direction. We packed up all of our shit, rented the U-Haul, and hit the road. There's not much to report about the drive except to say that it was long and boring.

By the way, what's the deal with New Mexico? Why the hell is that state so flat and miserable? I mean, think about it. I understand that Mexico sucks, but why would anyone name a state after another place, stick the word "new" in front of it, and make it even shittier? I'm a big advocate for the idea of selling New Mexico to a third world country for the price of a donkey-show admission ticket.

When we got to Arizona, the apartment building that we were all supposed to be moving into turned us away because it was only a three-bedroom, and that complex didn't allow a certain number of children to stay in one room. We had no place to go, and as brief as it was, I experienced my first homeless situation. The others would prove to be a lot worse.

I think we only stayed in hotels for a couple of days or so until my parents found a home to rent. Ironically enough, it was a three-bedroom home. I ended up sharing a fairly small bedroom with Jacob, Joshua, and Eli. Four freakin' boys in one room? That shit just ain't right, especially when you're fourteen and need that "personal time" to explore just who you really are. I'm talking about floggin' the dolphin for all you slow people in the audience.

My mother was always very organized and a strong advocate for education, and before I could blink, she had us registered for school and I was standing at the bus stop awaiting the first day of my new life. It was October, and I can tell you that it's a little chilly in Tucson in the morning waiting for the bus. I didn't expect that feeling. I got on the bus and would spend about two weeks not saying a word to anyone.

I *can* say this about the Tucson, Arizona's education system—they were WAY more advanced than where I was in Torrington. I left eighth grade studying fractions and shit and entered a school where the students were breezing through pre-algebra.

Please, parents, before you decide to move your kids to a new country (also known as Arizona) do some more research about the schools and what the teachers have on their lesson plans. To make matters worse, I had come from an area of the country where I could have elected to take Italian. That wasn't even offered in Arizona. The educational transition itself was the very first time I remember TOTALLY hating school. That feeling from then on would never subside.

Eighth grade in Arizona sucked. To keep my mind off of the fact that I was twenty-five hundred *plus* miles away from normalcy, I learned that there was a wrestling team. My father had wrestled in school, so I thought that would be something worth trying. I compare my talent on the wrestling team to Obama. It was kind of a good idea initially, but the outcome just proved to be unsuccessful and a waste of time.

I would go on to wrestle a couple more years with a similar outcome.

38

Mexico

My first realization that I would probably forever be a smartass, without fear of consequence, would come during my eighth-grade year. I was involved with a student exchange type of program where a student from Mexico would come stay with my family for a period of a few days, and then a month or so later, I would go down there and stay with his family.

His name was Ernesto, and he was a pretty cool kid. He didn't speak much English, but oddly enough, he could read and write it, so we just spent a few days writing each other letters back and forth in person.

When it was my turn to go to Mexico, I was totally excited. Ernesto lived in Magdalena, Mexico. Obviously it was a poor little town, but I mean *really* poor. The cool thing about it was that fireworks were legal. Well, I thought they were cool until a firecracker blew up in my hand. It hurt like hell and till this day, whenever I hear a loud noise, my right ear rings.

I remember going to school with him and wishing I lived there, because I was intellectually at the same level they were, and I'm sure I would have made all A's.

I remember going to my first night club and meeting a Mexican girl and learning that even though knowing Spanish would've helped me communicate more efficiently, there's something called *body language*, and that was a language that I could read very well. I don't know what it was, but the Mexican girls were lovin' me that night!

After a couple of days, the class left our gracious Hispanic hosts and got back on the bus. As a detour, we stopped near a small river for lunch and I got into an argument with a young local Mexican fisherman. I'm sure I was trying to pick a fight with the kid because I was a bit of a prick, and I always felt a need to show off to gain some sort of acceptance. Looking back on it now, I'm not sure who I was trying to show off in front of, because the class was still near the bus and I was alone.

Not realizing how far away I had drifted from the group to start this argument with Felipe[5] the kid's friends showed up, and with broken English tried to explain to me that they were going to beat me with an empty metal drum. I gave them the universal finger along, with a simple "Go fuck yourself," and turned around long enough to see one of the kids standing in front of me with an empty metal drum raised in the air above my head.

He didn't hit me with it, but just stood there laughing with his little friends.

I slowly moved past him and walked backward all the way to the bus.

I wouldn't return to Mexico for fifteen years.

---

[5] That's what I'm calling him … not sure why, but why not?

39

MY FIRST JOB

When wrestling season ended that year I wanted to get a job. Mexico was far behind me, and I felt wiser after experiencing a near-death Mexican burial. Funny thing is, I didn't care and would spend many years to come chancing death.

So, where does a fourteen-year-old kid go for a job? Well, on a street corner of course. Now before you start imagining a fourteen-year-old boy walking the streets, you sick fuck, I'm talking about selling newspapers. I found an ad in the paper looking for someone to work early mornings on the weekends selling the *Tucson Citizen*. It seemed like a really cool gig. I would wake up at the butt-crack of dawn, ride my bike a few miles to a parking lot meeting place, and take out a few bundles of newspapers on consignment. Then I would find a really good corner and walk back and forth with the newspaper proudly held in the air as if I was a ring girl at an old Sugar Ray Leonard fight (minus the bikini of course).

I didn't do too bad. Not realizing it until now, that was my first job in a sales-driven field. Although ... I think I'll leave that off my résumé.

Now, what I'm about to tell you has two different titles to it. I call it *the truth*, whereas my family calls it *bullshit*. I was minding my business early one morning, heading off to my first reason for financial existence when a hundred-pound coyote came out of nowhere and started chasing me.

I didn't know what was happening! All I heard was barking and then some paws smacking the pavement. I looked back just in time to see that son of a bitch trying to get himself some breakfast. Well, I wasn't ready to become some coyote's next meal, so I lit up those tires and took off as if my life was dependent on catching up to Lance Armstrong.

Now, since this book is written with as much honesty as humanly possible, I will say that during the Tour de Tucson, I screamed like a bitch the entire trip. Imagine Chris Tucker's voice with Cindy Lauper's lips. Very disturbing. After what seemed to be fifteen hundred miles, I lost the coyote, and my heart rate started climbing back down to a normal level. I got to work, grabbed my papers, and started my day.

I think about that coyote a lot. Partly because whenever that story gets mentioned, my parents laugh at me and tell me that I'm crazy. They say that there's no way a coyote was walking around a suburban neighborhood and deciding that he's going to grab some fast food and take off after me. Like that's not enough, they don't stop there. They actually do the opposite of what you're supposed to do over time after telling a story repeatedly. Usually a person starts off with describing something small, like let's say one dollar, and ends up at one million. My family likes to tell that story and instead of not believing me that their *only* third-born child was almost a wild dog's breakfast, they insist over time that the coyote was actually a dog, then it became a cat, then a kitten, then a shadow, and I'm pretty sure it's now just a figment of my imagination. Like I don't have enough problems as it is, I have my family telling me that I make up stories. Like I would *ever* do that!

Word got around that I had a job selling newspapers on the street corner, and my math teacher, Mr. What-Ever-His-Name-Was (I'll call him Mr. Billingsly) became fascinated by it. You have to understand that homeless people are usually the ones selling these papers on the street, not fourteen-year-old kids still in junior high. I talked about it a lot with him, and it seemed like he had a lot of respect for me for wanting to work hard.

One morning at work, I was in my usual spot— which was one of the better areas because it was an intersection in the midst of major fast food chains, grocery stores, drug stores, etc.—when a gentleman crossing the street came right up to me. He was a really big guy with a certain walk that I just couldn't place. It was as if he didn't have a care in the world and time stood still for him.[6]

He stood over me for what felt like hours and just stared. I wasn't sure what was going to happen, so I eventually broke the awkward silence and asked him if he wanted to buy a paper. He kindly said no, but asked if I believed in our Lord and Savior Jesus Christ. I wasn't as witty back then or I'm sure I would have answered with something like, "Sure Moses, I believe in him, would He like a newspaper?" Instead, I said yes and the man asked me if I would pray with him. Before I could do anything, he grabbed my hands and bowed his head murmuring words of faith and hope.

His grip was really strong, and I knew that I wouldn't be able to break it, so I just stood there staring at him, shocked at what was happening. Before I could come up with a plan on escaping, I heard tires squeal, brakes hitting hard, and a door slamming. I looked up to see my very tall eighth-grade math teacher running toward the intersection island. He had handcuffs in his hand, and he looked like a man possessed. When he got to us, Moses stood up and came face to face with the teacher.

Mr. Billingsly was ready for anything. He asked Moses if he knew me and instantly put the fear of God in him. Picking up on Mr. Billingly's sense of desire to get me out of there, Moses said that he didn't know me, but he felt that he needed to help me get closer to God. Mr. Billingsly didn't find the religious experience at the time to be that important and in so many words convinced Moses that he needed to find himself a different sea to part.

That was my last day selling newspapers and the first day that I realized people usually *(always)* have ulterior motives for demonstrating sincerity. The inappropriate shoulder massages from Mr. Billingsly would soon follow, and to this day, I can't accept a massage from anyone without feeling violated.

---

[6] Later in life it was a trait that I would grow to want.

40

The Rest of Eighth Grade

T o get my mind off of things, I poured myself into my studies. I tried to focus and do the best I could to reach the goal of being put on the honor roll. Unfortunately, I was bit by the Arizona bug of luck and missed it by a few points. I'm not sure if Arizona's grading system is supposed to be screwed up or they were just culturally biased because I'm Italian and not Mexican. Needless to say, I didn't make the honor roll, because an A is only an A above 92 percent, and a B is only a B above 84 percent. I was heartbroken. How could this happen? A huge part of me stopped caring the day those results became available.

The Dance

To get my mind off of things some more … I needed to settle down and pick out the lucky lady that would accompany me to the eighth-grade dance. I believed in the law of averages back then, like I do now, but figured that I would at least start at the top and ask the better-looking girls. If they said no, hey, I'd find someone to say yes.

I walked up to Diane, hands shaking, slightly less confident than I sound now, and introduced myself. She was really polite about the shaky introduction and asked me what was going on. I said not much, but that there was this eighth-grade dance thing coming up and ... if she wasn't busy ... I would really like to go with her. She smiled and said that she knew there was an eighth-grade dance, because she was planning on going, and she was in fact in the eighth grade. I was too nervous to understand that her sarcasm was an attempt to be cute, so I said forget it and angrily started to walk away. A few steps in, I was ready to find someone else when I heard her yell behind me to wait, and she ran over laughing. I asked her what was so funny and she said she was just messing with me and would love to go. I said okay and told her that I needed to get to class.

I was on top of the world. Not only was I going to my FIRST school dance with a really cute girl, but she had a funny sense of humor and seemed to really like the food I was serving. Unfortunately, not giving myself enough credit, I asked Diane to the dance too early, and the next time I saw her, she was holding my hand around campus and introducing me to people as if I was her boyfriend. That might not be the worst thing you've ever read, except back then the words, "My Boyfriend" triggered the sweat glands in my hands and made me beyond self-conscious about them.

After walking sweaty-hand-in-hand with Diane for about a week, I had to cancel the date. The embarrassment from the swamp-ass hands became too much to bear.

She wasn't happy with the news but took it like a champ, and I was a junior bachelor once again. My original plan of using the law of averages withered away with the constant memory of my leaky hands, and I would end up waiting until the last minute to ask someone else to go with me. As you can imagine, she wasn't the nicest looking girl out there. I mean, what did I expect? It's like waiting till two in the morning to start talking to someone at a bar. The pickings at that point are pretty slim.

Regardless of the fact that I settled on someone I wasn't really interested in, I went and had a pretty half-decent time. Of course at that time in my life, the Tootsie Roll dance was the most popular and really just not built for white people to master. So I did what every other self-respecting white guy does and waited for either a slow song to come on or the all-reliable electric slide.

There isn't a whole lot more to write about with regard to the eighth grade. I somehow graduated. I did what I do best and looked into how much work would need to be done to slip through the cracks and finish. I'm typically not the guy who finishes things, so to be able to say I completed something was pretty nice. I now wish I had the superhero power to see into the future. I know I would have enjoyed my eighth-grade graduation so much more if I had just known it would be the last time someone would hand me a certificate of completion.

41

My First Summer

H ot. What else can you say about it? As if everything I had been through up until that point hadn't yet convinced me that I was in hell, it proved to be hotter than hell could ever be. I remember leaving the East Coast listening to a lot of people saying, "Oh, it's hot, but it's a *dry heat.*"

My message to them is simple: "What the fuck do you know?" I don't care if it's dry heat or not, 120 degrees is still 120 degrees. It's like throwing a ghost pepper in with some sweet-and-sour sauce and telling people that it's not bad because it's like a sweet burn. Go ahead and try it—let me know how it works out for you.

To make matters even more exciting for me, one of my friends suggested that we go out for the football team. We did and ended up making the freshman team. This is an accomplishment I don't exactly hold dear to my heart for one simple reason—it was the freshman football team; they HAD to let you play.

Practices got to be a little on the hot side, and our team didn't like practicing during those temperatures, so as a punishment the coaches wouldn't let us take off any of our pads, *even* when we were on the sideline waiting to get into a play. I had to do something! I was driven by this uncontrollable urge to look out for my fellow teammates. First, I tried going up to the coach and nicely tell him that we should at least be able to take off our helmets. When that didn't work, and he made me do pushups for challenging his authority, I did what any fifteen-year-old kid would do: I explained to him very carefully that he was a dickhead.

Of course he didn't like that and after my next set of pushups, I was running laps … with my helmet on.

I enjoyed the run because it got me away from the situation and gave me time to think about how I could get back at this guy. About halfway through my run, I had a plan. I started running faster and faster to build up even more of a sweat. As soon as I crossed the point that ended the punishment, I continued running over to the coach and stopped right in front of him. He yelled, "What do you want Ventre?" I said nothing, but just simply fainted.

I wish I could have seen the look on that asshole's face, but I had to play it cool. I was going to show him the repercussions of his actions. I was pretending to be a heat casualty. I heard a lot of screaming, and the coach removed my helmet and was yelling for the medical team to come over. He started tapping my face, and I could hear in his voice that he was really nervous. So I opened my eyes very slowly. I called out for my mother, which I thought was maybe a little over the top, but the coach seemed to be buying it. They brought over water and carried me over to a shaded area, and I spent the rest of the practice watching a coach pace back and forth while the team stood on the sidelines without their helmets on. Go Jets.

42

Ninth Grade Here I Come

With the summer coming to a close, and many laid-back football practices behind me, I was ready for this thing called high school. How hard could it be? I figured that I wouldn't let it stress me out as much as I heard it did a lot of other people. Besides, I'd heard that everything you need to know, you learned in kindergarten, so the way I figured it, even if I dropped out of high school after the first day, I was still eight years above everyone else, right?

Having a birthday in August was really cool, because it seemed that every year I got one more new back-to-school outfit than everyone else. This year happened to be the best. White shorts, white cotton shirt, and a brown suede vest! I was stylin'! I had that outfit laid out on my bed weeks before school even started. Some nights I would actually change into it and check myself out in the mirror. Now I'm not gonna lie, I am rather attracted to myself, but I don't take that seriously because after all, I don't believe in incest.

To make the outfit even more exciting, I went to Payless Shoes and bought a pair of brown loafers, just so I could make the vest stand out even more. I was so ready.

As luck would have it, it rained the night before my first day of high school, and it was pretty muddy out there. Looking back on it now, I should have stayed home. Something that morning was trying to warn me, but I didn't listen. Besides, it's the first day of school, I'm supposed to go.

After my first class, I had to walk to the other side of campus to a bunch of trailers for math class. I had all of my books with me because I was very unfamiliar with the campus and I wasn't sure if I'd have enough time to get back to my locker. Some of the books fit in my backpack, while I carried the remaining four of them in my arms.

I was about twenty feet from the door to the math class trailer, when I lost my footing on some newly made mud and went feet over head like a clown looking for a laugh. Landing on my head would have normally been a reason to quit school right then and there. It's bad enough to have to learn math, but far worse to fall on your head. I picked myself up off the ground and naturally slipped again, this time landing on my face and chest.

I wanted to cry, to raise my fists into the air and scream at the Arizona God: "WHY?" I didn't though, and instead picked myself up off the mud-soaked ground and grabbed the four books that had somehow flew away from the mud and managed to stay relatively clean.

I was doing good. I kept telling myself that my books didn't get muddy and I could just wash myself off and be a little late for class. It's the first day, and I had a good excuse. Then it hit me. Reality. Dazed from the ground punching me in the back of the head and then smacking me in the front, I looked down and realized that my suede vest was dripping with rich Arizona mud. I lost control. I threw my books. I grabbed my backpack and threw that. I took off my shoes and threw those. Then, when I noticed that all my belongings had landed in a mud puddle, I threw up my hands and walked away.

I wasn't sure where I was going, but I was getting there fast. I noticed that at this point, I had an audience. Most of them had witnessed everything and I'm sure they didn't say anything to me for a couple of reasons:

1. What do you say to the guy that is throwing his shoes and school books all over the place?

And ...

2. The swear words that were coming out of my mouth while I was taking my journey were unprecedented. I even made up swears. I just didn't care at that point if people were unfamiliar with the definition of "knucklebuttshit."

I got to my destination, which happened to be the nearest bathroom, and I took off my vest and washed my face. I looked in the mirror, and for the first time all summer I didn't recognize myself. I looked older than I had remembered. Like I had figured out at too young an age that life isn't fair and my face had suffered the weather of it all. I had to figure out a way to compose myself, how to get my head back in the game. I took a deep breath, looked around the bathroom, had a quick cry and walked out. My socks were making noises because of how muddy they were as I walked toward the scene of the accident, but I didn't care. Besides, who wears socks with loafers anyways? When I arrived back at Mudville, I was surprised to notice that my belongings were still exactly where I had thrown them. That's Arizona for you. Either, someone will steal all your shit or they just won't help you out at all. I picked up my mud-soaked books, backpack, and loafers, and headed toward class.

When I got there, I took off my socks and cleaned off the shoes a little and prepared myself for algebra. I stood up, shook my head to clear my thoughts as if it was an Etch-a-Sketch and was about to walk in, when I noticed that without the brown vest, I was wearing a white shirt with white shorts and brown shoes. I also noticed the gigantic mud stains on my crotch and backside. I looked like a milkman who had just shit himself. I laughed out loud, thinking, *I'm just being silly and who's going to care to notice anyways?*

I walked through that door, and because I was so late for class at that point, everyone turned around, and then as if they were Olympic synchronized swimmers, their eyes all dropped to the brown stain on my crotch at the same time.

I sat in my chair thinking that life couldn't possibly get any worse.

Boy was I was wrong.

43

HIGH SCHOOL IS THE DEVIL

M y grades suffered immediately and I just knew that this whole high school idea was a bad one. I've never really been the kind of person who loved being in school. Actually, I've never really been the kind of person to like anything that is uniform and authority driven. Before I knew it, my grades were too low to play football, and I was asked to leave the team. In case you're wondering what my career stats were for playing wide receiver and special teams, well, let me see if I remember ...

0 tackles, 0 catches, 0 touchdowns, 0 wins.

Although, I do remember running into a guy once—not sure if we were on the same team or not; I was too busy thinking about that damn coyote.

With all this spare time on my hands, I started to hang around the football team off the field and primarily in the locker rooms. I would act like I missed practicing with them, and as soon as they hit the field for practice, I was breaking into their lockers and taking whatever I could.

I was never a really smart thief because whatever clothes I stole, I wore around campus. I was lucky enough to only have one football player come up to me and tell me that he used to have the same pants before someone broke into his locker. I panicked for a quick second and then asked him if he knew who could have stolen the missing pants, because I'm pissed off about it and would love to go kick that guy's ass for him. With that, he walked away.

I think about that conversation a lot and immaturely laugh to myself when I mentally relive my response to him. If I could turn back time, I probably would've told him I did steal his pants, but what's worse is the fact that I'm also wearing his underwear.

***

So eighth grade yielded zero possibility of selecting Italian for a language, and as upset at that as I was, I understood that Spanish is probably used more out there than Italian. But high school just *had* to be different. It's a level of education that should offer more possibilities, and I was confident that I would once again get the opportunity to learn Italian. I remember looking through the available classes—they had the normal stuff like Spanish ... and Spanish ... and French, and ... Spanish. No Italian. Big freakin' surprise! I ended up selecting French just out of spite.

Her name was Madam Lupont. She was a fiery redhead who started off the first class by telling the students a little bit about herself. Normally, I wouldn't really give a shit about the personal life of a teacher, because up until recently, they weren't really people to me. However, Madam Lupont had a husband, who unfortunately (at that time) had left her. The twist to the story and the main reason why I felt that Frenchie really need me was because Jerknuts not only left her, but he left her for another man.

I couldn't believe my ears! I mean, that was some serious Jerry Springer shit, and to top it off, she was telling her ninth-graders about it! She looked so sad. After a few upsetting weeks of watching this woman try to teach through such heartache, I needed to find a way to comfort her.

She came over to my desk one day and was trying to help me out with some French stuff, and I kindly asked her if she would ever consider having sex with one of her students. She didn't like that question and was really offended. I personally think that her attitude toward me and my innocent inquiry was just downright rude. How does this woman rationalize that telling fifteen-year-old kids about her frou-frou husband is okay, but what I asked her was wrong? Whatever. It didn't matter anyway, because with my numbered grade in that class running around a 19 percent, combined with what *some* might classify as harassment, would make that day my last one in Madam Lupont's classroom.

My stepfather was a six-foot-four Irish cop who worked the nightshift. I say Irish because they are notorious for having a hot temper, and I say the nightshift because there's no way you could get away with *anything*. That of course being because he didn't go to work until you were asleep.

At this point in my life, I had already been in Arizona for almost a year, and I would end up adopting the style of dress made famous by the locals. What I'm trying to say, is I was dressing like a beaner. I had the white jeans on with the white-and-black collared button-down shirt, with all of the buttons buttoned to the top.

I would walk in the door to see my stepfather sitting on the couch as if his life had meaning when he found out I'd done something wrong. We locked eyes. I could tell that he was looking at my outfit and probably wondering where I got it from. Of course, I wouldn't tell him the shirt was from some kid's locker and the pants ... well ... try not to laugh ... the pants were actually my sister's, but whatever.

My stepfather sat up and moved toward the end of the couch. He looked at me and said that he had received notification from the school about a certain comment that I had made toward one of my teachers. I knew that I was going to have to face this, but what I never imagined was to hear the words come out of his mouth that would paralyze me and make me forget to breath for a few seconds ...

"Jase, go wait in the garage for me."

I can confidently say that my stepfather was a genius for that move. I don't remember if I got the beating I probably deserved that day. A good beating is something that people usually remember, but what I do remember was worse than getting your ass kicked. He made me wait in that garage for him for at least thirty minutes. It seemed like an eternity. By the time he came in, I was ready to beat my own ass for my mistake. I don't really have anything against French people, but I do believe I felt a little less close to them that day.

44

WHAT THE HELL DID I DO?

My brother Jamie had decided at some point around this time that CT wasn't the best place for him to be and ended up making the move to AZ. As excited as I was to have my big brother back home, I had more important things to concentrate on. I still needed to master this thing we call, "High School."

One of my classes my ninth-grade year was Drama. I'm not even sure why I took it. I think the school should have just looked at the drama I brought into my life on a daily basis and instantly issued a credit. I hated it though. I had a hard time acting for some reason, although I don't know why because I'd spent my entire life acting, so what's one little class?

I was sitting in the auditorium one day when I overheard one of the upperclassman say that he couldn't wait for his jacket to come in. I asked him what jacket, and he told me that he knew a guy that could get NFL jackets pretty cheap. My heart started racing, my palms started sweating, and I started to imagine myself modeling the green and white. I asked him if he could get me a Jets jacket, and he said yeah, but it was forty bucks. I told him to order it, and I'd pay for it as soon as it came in. It was a stupid thing to say, because I didn't have forty dollars. I figured he would tell

me that I needed the money right then and there, but he didn't!
I walked out of that stupid class that day with my stomach in
knots.

The next day he didn't bring up the jacket, and I just chalked
it up to another kid talking shit. I thought I was in the clear, and
I wouldn't have to find a way to come up with money. A couple
of weeks later, though, long after I had already forgotten about
the stupid jacket, that kid walked in with a plastic bag. As if I was
wearing binoculars, I spotted the green and white through the
plastic from across the auditorium. He was holding up the jacket
and grinning. I couldn't believe it! He said that he needed to
collect the forty dollars and give it to his buddy. I told him that I
didn't have the money, but I'd bring it in tomorrow. He said okay
and tried to hand me the jacket.

I said that I didn't want to take it until I had the money (which
I figured I would never have and would probably just duck him for
a few days and then eventually apologize). He said not to worry
about it and pushed the Jets jacket bag in my chest and forced me
to take it. He played a perfect sales tactic. If you force the product
onto your prospective customer, then chances are, they are more
inclined to buy.

I went home that day shaking my head, knowing there was
no way my mother was going to give me the money because I had
already asked for the jacket, and I was sure she had planned on
getting it for me for Christmas. I got through dinner and went to
bed early knowing that what I would do next would take away the
part of a relationship that one should never be without.

The next morning I woke up very early for school, way before
the other kids, and got ready. When everyone else was distracted
by the hustle and bustle of a small house full of children, I made
my move. I went downstairs with the idea of just going into my
mother's purse and grabbing the money. Unfortunately, during
the robbery, I heard some noise and frantically just grabbed the
whole purse and threw it into my backpack. I walked around the
corner and took the cash out of her wallet and waited until the
noise I heard had gone away. I figured that I would just take the

purse back, but on the way back to the scene of the crime, the other kids were coming downstairs and I had to once again throw the purse back in my backpack ... fuck!

A few minutes before we would all leave to walk to the bus stop, my mother noticed that she couldn't find her purse and frantically asked us if we had seen it. Of course none of us had, and she would never have suspected that one of her kids would take her entire purse.

We left for school, and I met up with the kid I owed the money to and paid him. I felt ashamed for what I had done. What was supposed to be a simple dip for the cash, with a plan of returning the purse, had turned into a full-fledged purse snatch. There was no returning it now. I mean purses don't just hang themselves back up. It would raise too much suspicion. I had to get rid of the evidence.

With my brother living in Arizona in the tiny house with us, I had not only ripped off my own mother, but I'd also borrowed his clothes. I guess the locker-room jeans I now owned were just too dirty to put on my thieving ass, so why not steal my brother's?

During the class just before lunch, I also managed to steal a pair of scissors off my teacher's desk, and when the bell rang dismissing us to a land of greasy pizza, stale nacho's, and lunch-lady hairnets, I snuck off into the bathroom to try to rid myself of this rather incriminating evidence. I cut up all of my mother's cards, her ID, and any other pieces of information that could cause her more harm in the wrong hands. I then walked to a part of the school grounds that was desolate and threw the purse in the trash. I put the cut pieces of credit cards in my pants, because I was too paranoid to put them anywhere else.

The rest of the day was a blur. I kept thinking about what I'd done and wondered how they would ever find out. Except for the pocket full of cut-up credit cards and ID, there was no evidence. I felt bad for what I'd done, but was confident that I'd gotten away with it.

After school, I took the bus home. On the walk from the bus stop, I stopped in the desert because I had to take off my brother's pants and trade them in for the un-cool ones I had in my backpack. Because it's not like I could just walk in wearing his pants, take them off, thank him for *letting* me use them, and ask him to please discard the items I'd stolen from our mother. I had to think quickly. So, after changing into Poindexter's jeans, I placed my brother's jeans on the desert floor with a mental reminder to make sure I grabbed them for school tomorrow. I would figure out how to smuggle them back in the house sometime this weekend.

I walked in the house and saw that my mother was still upset about losing her purse. I overheard her saying that she had to cancel all her credit cards and now she was going to have to send away for all of her IDs. I couldn't handle the guilt, so I put on a concerned face, apologized for her loss, and went up to my room.

Unbeknownst to me, someone had seen me changing in the desert, and of all the people someone could hand that bit of information to, it went to my brother Jamie. Finding it to be odd, he went to investigate the informant's claim. Imagine his surprise while walking closer and closer to my hidden spot as realized that his initial thought of *Oh, those look like my jeans*, happened to, in fact, BE his jeans.

I was in my room enjoying the cool October air in my basketball shorts and a T-shirt, when I heard the door slam and my brother scream my name. I didn't know what was going on, but before I realized what was happening, Jamie turned into Superman and flew up the stairs. He came at me with a fury and forced me on the ground, yelling *"Thief!"* and swearing at me for stealing from his mother. I slipped away from his attack and sprinted out the door.

I was running through the desert as fast as I could. My heart was in my throat, and my legs started to burn. I couldn't run any further. I felt like I was going to collapse. I stopped for a few seconds to listen and see if I was being followed. For a few seconds, I thought I was in the clear, and then I heard my name being called. It was Jamie. He was relentless. I could see in the distance the beam of his flashlight.

I found a ditch and jumped in it, covering myself with as much dirt and brush as I could find, and lay there waiting to get caught. My brother's voice came closer and closer. At one point he stopped, and I heard him right above my head. He was pointing the flashlight straight ahead instead of downward, or I surely would have been caught. He eventually gave up and started walking the other way.

When I felt that the coast was clear, I got up, brushed myself off—cut and bleeding from the pine needles mixed in with my camouflage—and took off running again. When I got my bearings, I knew that one of my friends lived about a mile or so away from my current location, so I headed that way.

When I got to his house, I briefly explained the situation, and he said that there was no way I could stay there. He handed me a soda, a book, and a sheet off his bed and wished me luck.

I had nowhere to go, so I started walking through the desert again, because walking on the main streets was not the best idea. About an hour later, I came across a large cement pipe and crawled inside. I lay there curled up in the pipe, not believing where I was, and imagining myself spending the rest of my life in it. Before I knew it, I realized that I had to poop. I figured *why not?* and stepped out of the pipe, popped a squat, wiped my ass with the pages of whatever book my asshole of a friend gave me, and crawled back into my new home.

I wasn't able to sleep that much that night because even with the sheet, the cement pipe was a little uncomfortable, and I kept looking over to the dark side of the pipe imagining that at any moment a lion, tiger, or even a bear was going to come out and maul me.

Some people wake up to the amazing smell of bacon cooking on the stove. I awoke to the unique smell of my own shit sitting right next to me on the ground, topped by the first chapter of a novel I would never read. I laughed for a second and then realized where I was and what I had done. I had to get on the move. It was sure to get hot that day and sitting next to the desert ground was not going to do it for me. I put the sheet I had over the crap I took, and started making my way through the desert, away from my parents' house. I have no idea how far I walked that day, but I ended up in a different part of town and fell asleep in the shade at some park.

I woke up to my stomach really upset with me. I needed to find some food. I looked around the park and saw a family having a picnic. They were cooking some burgers and they smelled *delicidant.*[7]

I walked up to them and hungrily asked if they had an extra one. The father of the family looked at me, glanced at his wife, and said, "Of course." I was relieved that he said that because there was no way I was going to accept any other answer. I was a criminal on the run, and I was not going to let anyone get in my way. I sunk my teeth into that amazing piece of meat, and about halfway through, the questions started. I didn't want to tell them that I was low enough to steal my mother's purse, so I told that family a version of the story that made me seem like someone who had been framed. After eating lunch, they said that how my family was treating me was uncalled for, and they invited me to go home with them. Of course, I accepted and started to visualize my future with my new family.

Later that night after dinner, Mr. Newdad urged me to call home to see if I could talk some sense into my accusers.

---

[7] Yeah, I made that word up; it's a cross between decadent and delicious.

I reluctantly listened to my new, temporary father figure and dialed the number. My stepfather answered, and I tried to play it off like I didn't know why Jamie had attacked me and that this was just a misunderstanding. To my surprise, he didn't mention the cut-up credit cards in the pocket of the jeans. I immediately thought that maybe he didn't know about them, and that there was a possibility I could deny everything and get out of this mess. To test the waters, I told him that I was just really upset about the accusations. He said not to worry about it, and he would pick me up, and we would work through this. I gave him the address, and thirty minutes later, he pulled up to the house. I said goodbye to my new family and hopped in the car.

Trying to play it cool, I put myself in the mind-set of pure innocence, ready to deny everything. He played it cool until we got home. I walked in the door, and there waiting for me was exhibit A, the stolen jeans.

I immediately went into denial mode and said, "What? Those aren't my jeans." Then I saw next to them, the credit card pieces. The jig was up. My mind went blank.

I wish I could tell you what the punishment was, but I honestly don't remember. I'm sure it wasn't good. To this day, every time I see a woman in passing wearing a purse, a feeling of overwhelming guilt fills my head, and I wonder when we look at each other if she's thinking that I might steal it.

45

THE PLAN

Things were getting to be a little too heavy, and I realized at that point that there was no way I could ever live down my mistakes in that house. So what does a fifteen-year-old kid in my position do to forget about what he had done? He runs away, that's what.

Before locking in that decision, I had to weigh what was going on. I made a mental list that I'm sure looked a little something like this:

Now as you can see, the amount of thought I put into my new plan was enough to make an educated decision. After making my

The Good in Arizona	The Bad in Arizona
I had some family in Arizona	The majority of my family was not in Arizona.
	It was too hot.
	Too many Mexicans, not enough Italians.
	My biggest mistakes were there.

list, I hadn't just decided to run away; I came to the conclusion that I *had* to run away. There was no other way out. I had shamed my family and ruined my name. It was time to go.

The next day at school was when it was going to happen; I just had to find a way to escape. I looked at my assets and found that I didn't really have any. I had no cash, no credit cards, no bank checks, and no ID. Normally, that would have stopped someone from starting a new life, but not me. My father had moved to Marietta, Georgia, with his new family, and after visiting him there last Christmas, I believed with my whole heart that if I could just find a way to get there, everything would be all right.

I stayed awake that night imagining the tears rolling down my father's face as he gave me a big hug and welcomed me home. The hug would last forever, and during it, he would assure me that I was safe. He would promise me that my life would be filled with love and support from this point on. It was a feeling that I didn't have in Arizona.

I remember lying there that night knowing without a doubt that Georgia was my destination and come hell or high water, that's where I was going. Of course, I had to figure out how to get there. A plane was out of the question, because I didn't have any money to pay for a last-minute ticket. A train was too expensive, and hitchhiking left too many uncertainties. I knew at that point that the only way to get there was to take a bus.

I had made my decision and quietly removed my school books from my backpack. I replaced the books I hadn't learned anything from with the bare necessities. Some clothes, toothbrush, toothpaste, deodorant. This was a true high-school boy's survival pack.

I hopped on the school bus, and as it drove off, I looked out the window, positive that it was the last time I would ever see that shithole. I was a free man. Free from the hassles and stress of suburban slavery. I laughed inside like a diabolical super villain, and then looked around the bus really quick to make sure that no one heard me laugh, and laughed again when I reminded myself that I hadn't laughed out loud.

Realizing that I was getting too excited for my trip, I concentrated on slowing my breathing. I was excited, but there were too many holes in my plan at this point. I had decided to bus across the country, but I didn't have any money; I didn't have the bus schedule, and I didn't have any way to get to the bus station. I had to think. I closed my eyes and concentrated. Ten minutes later I had come to three conclusions:

1. How the hell could the Jets have drafted Kyle Brady? According to me, we had a very strong need at quarterback, and considering that Boomer Esiason was not the guy that would take our team to the next level, why not go after a young kid that we could mold into an elite NFL quarterback?[8]
2. I can't believe that the *Calvin and Hobbs* comic strip has ended.[9]
3. I don't care what those moronic jurors came up with, OJ Simpson, is not innocent.

I nodded and gave myself quick acknowledgment at my ability to come up with random events that remain active in my brain, and when I looked up we were in front of the school. I bounced back to reality. I was nervous again. My mind was made up, but I had once again let my mind wander. I still didn't have a solid plan on how I was going to pull this off.

I started walking toward my locker, and the smell of cinnamon rolls filled the air. I wanted one so badly. I reached into my pocket like I did every day, hoping that the money fairy had snuck a few dollars in there as I slept. Wrong again.

I reached into the other pocket and pulled out a few coins. Score! I had enough money for the cinnamon roll, but I had to conserve funds. I knew at some point I would have to call and get the bus schedule, so my newly found fortune would go toward

---

[8] I am clearly still upset about it.

[9] I would continue to stay concerned about that for a number of years.

that. I went up to the cinnamon roll woman and told her that our house had just burned down and my family had nothing. I explained to her as I held my stomach that we were starving and hadn't eaten in days. I would have gone into more horrible poverty-stricken details, but tears started to fill her eyes and she handed me a cinnamon roll, asking me not tell anyone. I thanked her and went on my way.

I got to my locker, put my book bag in it, and then sat on the ground leaning up against it enjoying my sweet breakfast. Every bite I took melted into the sticky frosting and collapsed into the warm soft bread. I devoured it with the precision of a surgeon. Afterward, I burped and realized that I still had yet to come up with any type of plan. I needed to walk, clear my head, gather my thoughts, but there was no time. I needed to report to homeroom. They did roll call early in the morning during homeroom, so I definitely couldn't miss that.

During homeroom I sat there and started devising my plan. On a piece of paper I made a list:

1. Look up number to the bus company. Call and get schedule and price.
2. Raise some money.
3. Get to the bus stop.
4. Get on the bus.
5. Sleep until I get to Georgia.

My plan made sense. It was simple. It was strong. It was mine.

After homeroom, I ran to the nearest phone booth, but there wasn't a phonebook on it. Damn! I then went to the office and asked the front desk woman if I could borrow her phonebook. When she wasn't looking, I jotted down the number and then quickly went to the auto section. When she turned around, I made sure she noticed me dramatically rip out the page. I put the book on the counter, thanked her and left.

I thought I was a genius. When the shit hit the fan, I would be halfway across the country; my parents would investigate, and I'm sure that woman would come forward and say that I was in fact acting a little weird. I imagined her grabbing the phonebook and finding the place where the missing page was. Everyone would think that I was trying to buy a car, and that would put them on the wrong path, never suspecting me to be on a bus.

I went to the payphone and called the bus company. The only bus they had leaving for Georgia wasn't until around six or so. That wasn't good, but I didn't have a choice. I got the price, and now I just needed to find a way to raise the money.

I went up to a friend of mine and struck up a conversation in a really depressed voice. Naturally, he asked me what was wrong, and I told him that I was going through a lot at home, and I was just really upset about it. I could see the concern in his face, and I felt bad about lying to him, but I had no choice. He was a really popular kid, and I knew that if anyone had the networking capabilities of raising some money for my next adventure, it was him. He asked if everything was okay. I said no, shed a tear, and told him that my stepfather was smacking me around a little too much, and I needed to get to Georgia to be with my real father before things got bad. I then told him that I was ready to go, but I somehow misplaced my wallet containing my limitless fortune and now I was screwed.

He said, "Don't worry about it. I will find a way to help you."

We shared third period together, and by the start of it, he had raised $200 for me! I was ready. All I needed to do now was somehow get to the bus stop without being detected, buy my ticket without raising suspicion, and then ride off into the sunset. Or sunrise, as it were.

I didn't want to leave too early because I was afraid that too many missed classes would evoke a reaction from the front office, and a phone call would be made. But at the same time, the bus stop was over ten miles away, and I needed to get started at some point. Estimating that I could walk a mile in about fifteen minutes, I needed to leave about four hours before my scheduled departure so I could have a little bit of a buffer. I figured that I would leave right after they did roll call at the beginning of fourth period so I would have plenty of time to get there.

I said goodbye to my buddy, checked in to my next class, and when the teacher wasn't looking, I snuck out the door, walked off campus, and into the desert. I stayed parallel with the road, but out of sight. The really cool thing about Tucson is that the roads are really easy to understand, so I had a good idea of how to get where I was going. After a couple of miles, I started to get tired. I wanted to sit down and take a nap, but I knew I had to get to my destination. It started to get pretty warm, and I knew that I hadn't had anything to drink all day. I needed to find water or things could get ugly.

I walked out of the desert at a place where there was a gas station across the street. I had plenty of money, so buying water wasn't going to be a problem. I walked in, and on the way to the water cooler, I passed some bread. Thinking that it would be a good idea to buy some for the trip, I picked it up and grabbed two bottles of water. I drank one of them immediately, but brought the empty one up to the counter with me not really understanding why, because after all, I was a thief. Nonetheless, I paid for both waters and the bread and left the store.

I went back to my ending point in the desert and continued walking. After some time, I started running out of desert and knew I was going to have to take to the streets. A few miles later, I started to tire again. I drank some more water and tried to occupy my mind away from the fact that I wasn't even at the halfway point yet. I started thinking about my time so far in Arizona and all of the things that had happened. Then I thought of the coyote, quickly looked behind me, and then decided not to think at all anymore.

I got to the bus stop sometime around four o'clock. I had made great time, but now there was too much time before the bus was going to leave. I went up to the counter, bought my ticket with my high school ID and sat down. Two hours was going to be a long wait, but I didn't have a choice.

I started talking to a gentleman next to me, and he seemed like a nice enough guy to tell my life story to. He seemed interested at first, and then I told him half-jokingly that my stepfather was a cop and any minute now they would realize that I wasn't there. He started to shift in his seat uncomfortably and I didn't know why. So as not to pry into his life, I stopped talking.

When the bus arrived, I waited anxiously for the passengers to get off, so I could get on. I was so excited. I had gotten away with it, and any moment now, I would be faced with the reality that the only thing between me and my father was open road. I was snatched out of my daydream by my new friend telling me that he just saw a police car pull up. I started to shake. No way could that be my stepfather. I'd covered my tracks so well, hadn't I? My friend told me to go around the back near the buses and try to hide. I did.

A couple of minutes later, the cop car pulled around and stopped right in front of me. The door opened and out stepped my stepfather. He told me to get in the car. I climbed into the back. He got in, and the swearing began. It was odd to be riding in the back of a cop car again, but I was glad, because there was a protective Plexiglas barrier separating me.

46

JUVENILE HALL

irst, he started telling me that the guy I was talking to was a known child molester. I didn't believe him, and after what seemed like an eternity of lectures and swears, swears and lectures, we arrived at our destination. I looked out the window and didn't remember my mother's house looking that way. Then it hit me, I was at a juvenile detention center. What the hell was he going to book me for? Underage bus boarding? This was ridiculous, and I started to become wildly annoyed.

He opened the car door and then escorted me through the door of the center. He had a plan. He was going to scare me.

I sat down with him and a counselor, and they tried to work out an understanding that running away from home was illegal, and combined with all the other bad decisions I was making in my life, I was surely going to end up here. I didn't really care that much though, because after all, the lobby didn't look that scary.

They took me on a tour of the junior inmates. I looked through the small glass peephole of their little rooms. I saw them pacing around looking back at me as if they were hoping I'd open the door and they could kill me. I'm sure that was what my stepfather was going for: the hope that I would develop a fear that would inevitably make me turn over a new leaf and instantly become a better student, sibling, and child. I would go on to excel at school and sports, to get both an academic and sports scholarship. Then I would go on to play ball for Notre Dame, then on to Harvard for my doctorate degree, eventually becoming a neurosurgeon.

We then went back to the counseling room, and I couldn't take it anymore. Too many words of a positive future were being thrown at me. I started to think about that room and their desperate attempt to scare me with the reality of what it would be like to have to live in it. But what I saw when I looked in that room was one kid or two at the most. A toilet, a bunk bed, and what looked to be a quiet environment. Then I compared that room to my current room of four boys, a toilet in the hallway that I shared with seven other people, and a whole lot of noise.

I thought to myself, *How nice would it be to go to jail to get away from the family.*

When I snapped out of it, I looked up to see that a response to the concerns of the counselor and my stepfather was needed, so I told them that I would try to do much better, I wouldn't run away anymore, and that I was sorry. With that response, I was taken home. I went to my room, lay on the bed, closed my eyes, and started mentally preparing the next escape.

47

DO YOU WANT FRIES WITH THAT?

My ninth-grade year was coming to a close, and I would soon find out that I had racked up enough credits to once again graduate from *the eighth grade*. Aside from the freshman version of gym, I'm pretty sure I didn't pass any other class. I can't say that I was devastated, because after all, I knew that I wouldn't go on to become a scholar and solve the world's oil shortage problem by inventing a new fuel that runs off of babies' tears. I just figured that I was destined to pump gas or drive a delivery truck, you know, something exciting.

My sister Kellie graduated from high school that year, which was awesome because my grandparents were going to come all the way out from the East Coast for it. They rented an apartment somewhere in Tucson, and I spent a good deal of the summer with them. It was like old times, and for about a month or so, I felt like I was home again. (Even if it was a ridiculously hot version of it.)

Unfortunately, all good things do have to come to an end, and they left. I was once again stuck with the reality that I was in freakin' Arizona, it was hot, and I needed to find a way out.

My living situation at that time wasn't the most uncomfortable, because we were finally moving into the new house my parents bought. I would get my own room for the first time. I was totally excited about it. I could just close the door and flex my forearms whenever I wanted to without the concern of anyone walking in. No more midnight solo bathroom romancing for me. I was ready for the big time!

I helped them pack the house and move all of the stuff a few miles down the road to our new digs. It was a beautiful home: traditional Southwest styling with the adobe tile roof, a three-car garage, five bedrooms, the works.

When we settled in, I felt it was important to venture into the real world and find a job. It would be my first real job since the newspaper incident of '94, and I felt that I was ready to jump back into the workforce. After all, cross-country bus tickets didn't grow on trees.

I wasn't sure where I wanted to work; all I knew was that I wanted to find a company that believed in me and could offer me a chance to better myself with room for advancement into a possible career in upper management. I searched for many seconds until my eyes rested on those amazing, beautiful yellow arches. It was Mc-E-Dees for me! That building stood out to me like a pot of gold to an Irish midget.

I walked in the door, filled out an application, asked to speak with a manager, and demanded a job. I wasn't leaving there until I was given the upper-middle-class role of official Major Food Group Acrobatic Engineer—burger flipper, for short.

After the manager witnessed my commitment, he naturally offered me the position, and after negotiating my pay all the way up to minimum wage, I came to two conclusions:

1. My future will not take me to a place where I will be in charge of salary negotiations.

And ...

2. I had made it. I could cross McDonalds peon off of my bucket list.

That summer yielded a lot of changes in me. Because of my friends, I started to really get into country music, and I promised myself that when I received my first paycheck, I would go buy my first pair of Wrangler jeans. I was totally excited. I would become an Italian cowboy. How cool was that?

All right, all right, I never said that I *still* think it's cool, but back then I was trying to find myself, and on payday I happened to find myself in K-Mart trying on a shiny new pair of the snug pants, or as I now like to call them, Cowboy Leggings. The problem with buying a pair of cowboy jeans was the fact that I had grown quite a bit taller that summer, and I was skinnier than the *Before* picture of an adopted Angelina Jolie baby. You'd think that after trying on these ridiculous jeans with a size 27 waist, I would stop, drop, and roll—hoping to put out the embarrassing teenage crisis that I was going through. Nope. I was doing this, and it would be a transformation that would haunt me for years.

The major issue with these particular K-Mart specials I was now wearing was the length. They didn't actually have the size that I needed, so the waist was super tight, showing off my first sign of a predominant donkey knuckle, but it appeared that I was also wearing high waters. Because money was tight and my first paycheck netted an astonishing $200 or so, I couldn't go to the mall and pay more for a size that would grant me the length I needed. I had to settle on these because I still had to buy boots.

Sneakers weren't going to do it for me. Naturally K-Mart didn't have authentic cowboy boots, but my newly reformed cowboy friends insisted that the mid-top black work boots were just as good, so I picked up a pair of those. I felt good about my selection, but I needed something to top it off.

So, I picked up my last item in an attempt to pull the outfit together: a belt buckle. Now this wasn't your ordinary run-of-the-mill belt buckle. Oh no. This thing was made of a cheap metal and then coated with a shiny, imitation silver material making it scream, "Look at me!" Of course, if you did look at it, you would notice the equally shiny plastic spur in the middle that in fact, DID spin. Despite the fact that my parents and siblings would try to convince me not to wear those pants by telling me that they were too tight and would affect my chances for procreation, I wore them proudly. Jason Ventre had gone country.

For my sixteenth birthday, I was given a bunch of cowboy apparel. I received a couple of belts that only someone who can successfully pull off Wranglers could get away with wearing. They were made of some sort of twisted plastic material. One was blue and one was red. I decided not to sport any of them because after all, I wasn't an advocate for the Bloods *or* the Crips.

The one gift I was totally excited about though—at first—was the *authentic* cowboy hat I received. Unfortunately, because of the fact that my head is the size of a lima bean, when I placed the hat on my head, I resembled Fievel, the star of *An American Tail*. This was a great movie, and I catch myself humming the main song of it from time to time, but let's face it, I'm not a mouse, so I couldn't wear the hat.

Aside from that, my sixteenth birthday wasn't anything to write home (or in this book) about. There was a cake, a bunch of siblings singing something to resemble the Ballad of "Happy Birthday" and that was about it.

48

The Permit

I was really enjoying my new life in the fast-food industry, and at one point I wanted to change my last name to McDonalds. I had learned all the inside scoop on how they prepared the food and would eventually come to believe that I was the best at it. I had a certain Processed Burger Flip Technique that I felt was unmatched.

I worked my ass off at that job, and when I wasn't at work, I was walking around the neighborhood showing off my cowboy leggings as if I were a freakin' runway model.

To take a break from the pro-bono modeling gig, I was preparing diligently to take my driver's permit test in hopes of one day getting a license, buying a car, and perhaps driving away from this god-awful place.

I was never good at taking tests, no matter how prepared for them I was. There's just something about them. I freeze up. I'm a little better with oral exams, but the problem with them is that I get anxiety from being in front of someone and not wanting to get the answer wrong. I'm all kinds of messed up.

The first time I had failed the permit test wasn't really a big deal. I felt that I had studied, but the best way for me to really learn something is to get it wrong a couple of times, so I had figured that would happen. The second time I took it, I didn't know the answer to the first three in a row and said, "Fuck it," picked random answers for the rest of the test, and then walked past the counter waving goodbye and telling the lady I would see her tomorrow.

In preparation for the third attempt, I studied all night. I had to pass this time because if you fail three times, you have to wait six months to retake the test. I was determined that nothing was going to get in my way of that piece of paper granting me the freedom to drive a vehicle, supervised, during daylight hours.

I had never studied harder in my life. I got to a point where I felt that if I had to, I could rewrite that entire DMV booklet front to back. I could teach a class about it and then maybe even get a job leading safety seminars all over the state!

My friend and his mother wanted to drive me to take the test the next day, and I said of course. I knew that when I passed, I would be able to drive home, and I also knew that if they drove me, I was sure to get some food out of the deal. They loved to eat. They also had a really cool conversion van that I was dying to take out on the road.

I walked up to that building, saw the enormous DMV letters, laughed at the thought of it really standing for the Devil's Mighty Vagina, and went inside. I was immediately disappointed when I didn't get a different vibe from before. I thought that after all that studying, I would thrust open the doors, and a gigantic wind blowing my scarf behind me would force everyone to turn around and see me standing there in my pilot suit and all my glory. I thought a group of admirers would carry me over to the testing center and sit me down on a pillow, while three gorgeous women fanned me and fed me grapes and a ten-year-old Nigerian boy handed me a new pair of Nikes as a gift. I'm not sure why he would do that, but why the hell not? This is my dream, not yours.

Nope, no gust of wind. No looks of admiration. No scarf. No pilot suit, women, grapes, or Nikes. I stood there embarrassed for a second, with my head down, looking at my horrible K-Mart work boots and suddenly got upset that I had made that purchase. I had to focus my mind now. No time to feel sorry for myself.

I checked in with my old friend, Barbara, at the front desk. We were now on a first-name basis. She asked me if I was ready this time. I snickered at her. Who was she to challenge the level of vehicular knowledge I now possessed? I said of course I was ready, gave her an arrogant wink, and started the test.

Ten minutes later, I had failed again. My hopes of one day becoming a delivery driver were starting to dwindle.

I walked out of that building with my head down, refusing to accept the fact that I had failed. Was EVERY test in Arizona culturally biased? What did the Italian community EVER do this this state? My friend's mother gave me a big hug, and I wanted to cry. She looked at me with sad eyes and felt my disappointment. I looked back at her and misread the look she had for pity and instantly thought that she was looking at me like I was some sort of dummy. I pushed her arms off me, walked out the door, punched a newspaper dispenser, and got in her van.

What sucks about this particular drive home was in fact that van. The whole ride home was a gigantic reminder that I had failed, because I wasn't driving it. I had an uncontrollable feeling that came over me telling me that I should just steal that van and show her. Who the hell does she think she is comforting me and showing that she cares? I was clearly upset at the wrong person. I was then broken out of my vengeful thoughts by the beautiful view of the Dairy Queen sign. She knew my weakness, and it just wasn't fair.

I got home, walked in the door, bypassed the false, family pleasantries, and went straight to my room.

It was the summer of '96, and I kept all of the newspaper clippings of the summer Olympics pinned up, primarily of the track star, Michael Johnson. I thought he was awesome with his shiny gold shoes. I looked at his photos and asked him why, as if he had something to do with my inability to pass written tests. Of course he didn't answer, so knowing I had to work that night, I took a nap thinking the only thing that could be worse than what had just happened to me was to dream of it happening all over again, but luckily for me that *didn't* happen.

49

GRADE 9.2

Another year of high school was about to start, and I
was a different man. I went from Jason Ventre, the
underachieving runaway freshman with no identity
to Jason Garth Brooks McDonalds, the hard-working, burger-
flipping sophomore cowboy.

Of course, in reality, I didn't have enough credits to really be
considered a sophomore, but who's counting?

I was excited to show off my new look and extensive knowledge
of country music. There were a couple of girls who were sure to
appreciate my new look. They were interesting creatures called
cowgirls. They wore big hats, boots, ridiculously large belt buckles,
and those jeans with no pockets in the back. You know the kind.
Snuggy. A year ago, I didn't have what it took to talk to these girls.
I listened to rap music and dressed like I was riding shotgun on
a drive-by shooting. These girls wouldn't have gone for that, but
now I had a shot. I was excited to talk to them.

I was also excited because I was going back to high school as a
working man. I had money in my pocket, so I didn't feel like I had
to ask for everything. I was my own man. If I wanted a cinnamon
roll, I was going to buy one. No more conning anyone. I also had
enough money saved that in the event I needed to leave, I would

be able to do so, but the most exciting part of that second year of high school—dance! I can't stress enough how excited I was about this class. When you're a freshman in this high school, you are forced to take gym class—also known as team sports—but your second, third, and fourth year, you can opt to take dance instead. When I first learned about this idea, I thought about it for about a second. I needed to dip down deep into my teenage psyche and weigh the odds. I would ultimately make a decision based on the outcome. I sat down and made a list:

Gym Class	Dance Class
Fun sports to play	Girls
Smelly guys	Girls in leotards
Showering next to smelly guys	Girls
Lots of running	Bumping and grinding with girls
30 guys and maybe 10 girls	30 girls and 1 guy

From that list I came to two conclusions that day:

1. I'm signing up for dance class.

And

2. I'm not gay.

My thought behind being the only guy willing to take a dance class with thirty girls was almost spot on. I signed up for the class and found out that only one other guy was in that class besides me. His name was Malik or Jameriqua or something, but what was important was that I was going to learn to dance hip-hop and start a new craze across the nation. Hip-Hop Country. It was going to be huge; I just knew it.

The night before school started, I said a little prayer. Nothing too big, but I just prayed to have a better first day than last year.

Anything would be better than that day, which I now nickname "The Day of the Freshman Folly."

Mr. Jesus apparently was awake that night, because the first day of school went by without incident. I got a lot of comments on my new look and a lot of new looks from the girls wearing the tight jeans without the pockets in the back. I thought to myself that they are all probably staring at me wondering what tumbleweed blew in the new hot cowboy. I smiled as I walked by them, almost taunting them to say something so I could wow them with my new country persona. They checked me out from top to bottom and just when I didn't think their smiles could get any bigger, they stopped at the bottom where my jeans that were too short, and came to a rest on the top of my black work boots. Then they turned around and didn't look anymore. Damn you, K-Mart, for your cheap prices and limited selection!

I was a little upset when the cowgirls didn't jump all over me, screaming "Give it to me, you Italian stallion," but it wasn't going to ruin my day. I still had dance class to look forward to, and based on my sister's critique of the same class she'd taken a year before, it was going to be a lot of hip-hop dirty dancing. I couldn't wait.

With my luck having it, the teacher that taught it the year before was replaced with a different one. The new teacher, Mrs. Boringhips, excelled in the dance style most commonly known as ballet.

I was devastated. It was as if life took away my god-given manly right to dance all sexy with a girl and replaced it with a tutu. My dreams were once again crushed. I didn't care about any of the other classes I was in that day or the cowgirls or my shorts Wranglers. I walked through the halls like a man with no soul.

How silly could it be that I was feeling that low? How could something so small change my entire mental perception? They were questions that I had that would go years before anyone could answer them for me.

50

ALMOST THERE

The first month of school went by pretty quick. I was working up to thirty hours a week at the restaurant, going to school, and rehearsing the dance routines with the different groups I was placed in. I had a lot on my plate, but my home life wasn't really where I felt it should be. I still didn't feel that it was healthy. I wasn't getting abused. I was being fed and a roof was over my head, but there was something about it that just didn't feel right. My life was heading in a tolerable direction, but something wasn't there. I needed to figure out what was missing.

It took another month before I would figure it out. Without realizing it, I was covering up my distain toward Arizona with activities. Those activities were keeping my eyes shut to the fact that I was in a place I hated, and my father, a man I loved, was somewhere else. A wave of goose bumps covered my skin, and the adrenaline rush from my latest epiphany made me start to shake. I knew what I needed to do and what would make me happy.

I needed to be with my father and as far away from Arizona as I could get.

Nothing else mattered to me. When I found the grass to be greener in Georgia, I stopped caring about my job, I stopped caring

206

about my dance class friends, I stopped caring about everything. I became a planning tactician, like a death row inmate obsessed with breaking out of prison. I knew without a shadow of a doubt that my life was going to be better with my father. I was back to planning my escape.

I called up the airline and found out that the ticket was $300. I had the money and felt so relieved that, financially, I had already left. Then I called up one of my friends, and one day after school, we drove down to the airport and purchased my airline ticket, set to leave one week later. All I had to do now was get through seven days without raising suspicion about my new plan to fly away from the cuckoo's nest.

I can now safely say that my ability to hide emotion and planning through a smile was sparked by that last week. I unknowingly became a student of convincing someone that life is great, but behind the scenes, planning something that would completely contradict those statements.

That week was difficult for me. Trying to pull the wool over the eyes of a cop made me feel like an amateur chess player going up against Bobby Fischer. But I couldn't lose; I couldn't get caught this time. The embarrassment would be too great. I didn't want to give him the satisfaction. Before I knew it, the day had arrived. I was going to get out of there, and knowing that, gave me the courage to continue with my plan.

I went to school that day not giving a shit about anything. I looked up at the teachers thinking to myself that I would never have to see their faces again. I would never have to complete one of their moronic assignments again. I wanted to shout at them that their boring and unimaginative ways of teaching is what was killing the educational system in this country. On any other day, I probably would have, but I had to keep control over the fire that was starting to build in my chest. I couldn't do anything that would keep me from reaching my goal.

After seven classes and lunch, I was done with that school and hopped in my buddy's car. He drove me home. I had my luggage already packed, but I couldn't bring everything with me because after all, a bare room just might tell a parent that her kid is gone and she might want to go look for him.

I told my mother that I had to work that night, and when she was in the bathroom, I smuggled my packed belongings out the front door and into the trunk of my buddy's car.

I dressed up in my McDonald's uniform and headed out the door. I got into my friend's car, pointed straight ahead, and said, "To the airport, my good man."

51

Snitches and Bitches

I checked in at the front desk using my high school ID card and received my itinerary. Looking down, I noticed that I had a layover in Las Vegas. How cool is that? A sixteen-year-old kid going to Vegas!

As much as I loved McDonald's, it was time to change out of my uniform and slip into something a little more comfortable. I went into the restroom and removed the secret outfit I had in my backpack and changed into it. When I walked out of the stall, I looked up to see my reflection in the mirror. I liked what I saw. He was not only a handsome young man, but someone who looked older to me. Wiser. I saw a man who had set out to do something and he was going to get it done. I felt close to him. I looked up to him.

I discarded my McDonald's uniform on the way out of the bathroom and headed toward security. I wasn't scared anymore. I wasn't even nervous. I was a little anxious at the thought of having to call my father when I got in to say, "Hey, Daddy guess what ..." But I would worry about that later. I was on my way to Georgia via *Viva Las Vegas!*

I got through security with no problems and headed over to my gate. With every announcement made with regards to my flight, I felt closer to reaching my goal. I eventually boarded and the plane took off. Forty-five minutes later, I was flying over the Las Vegas strip, and the lights were mesmerizing. It was like the Jersey Shore for big people ... minus the shore. I fantasized for a few seconds on what it would be like to just get off the plane in Vegas and become a professional gambler. I'd seen movies about them, and it was a life seemingly filled with excitement and danger. Two things that were clearly right up my alley. I decided that now wasn't the time for that type of fun and watched as the plane touched down on the runway.

I had an hour layover in LAS, and then I was off to Atlanta. My life in Arizona was behind me, and in six short hours I was going to have to make the call to my father. I didn't want to think about that just then, so I had to find something else to take my mind off that certainty. I walked over to a slot machine and tried to put some quarters in it. It wouldn't work. My money kept falling out the bottom. Security came over and asked if there was a problem. Yeah, if he only knew. Imagine the look on his face if I told him my life story, where I was from, what I'd been through, what I'd done, and to top it off, I could end my life summary by telling him that now I was trying to gamble underage. Instead, I tried to act a little older and knowledgeable in the world of gambling and said, "Uh, yeah this machine is clearly broken."

He told me that the machine didn't take quarters. He then said that not many machines out there did anymore. I shook my head, looked up at him, and said, "Wow, how things change. Back in my day, these machines used to take nickels. It's horrible getting old isn't it?" He shot me a quizzical look, so I quickly turned around and walked away.

Figuring that my underage gambling career should probably be put on hold, I went back to my gate and sat down. It was difficult just sitting there, because my adrenaline was pumping a little too fast to stay calmly seated for the next forty-five minutes. I had to do something. I was about to crawl out of my skin!

Sitting next to me was a young, attractive woman and her husband. They couldn't have been more than thirty years old. I struck up a conversation with them. They were well-spoken and excited about their trip back home to Atlanta. I was happy for them, but really didn't care too much about what they were saying, because I had my own thoughts to get off my chest. The couple asked about me and where I was heading. I told them that I was going to go live with my father in Georgia. I said that I was really excited about it because I hadn't seen him in a little while and my life was going to be great there.

With a smile, the woman said, "Oh, that's nice. I bet he's happy too."

I said, "I'm sure he *will* be happy, but he doesn't know that I'm coming. It's a surprise."

At that point, the conversation ended, and I didn't understand why she had a worried look on her face. She got up and left while her husband moved over into her seat next to me and sat there, not saying a word. It was awkward. I didn't understand what her problem was and why this guy was so close to me. The tension got to be too much, and because I couldn't place where it was coming from, I decided to walk around for a few minutes. As I got up and took a few steps forward, I was stopped by a couple of airport security guards asking me to follow them.

At first I said no, but they insisted. I knew I didn't have a choice, but just couldn't figure out what their problem was. I briefly imagined myself in an interrogation room trying to act tough.

I knew they would break me and eventually force me to confess that I was attempting to use one of their slot machines illegally. With that thought, they sat me down in a room and a few minutes later, two police officers came in and told me that the woman I was sitting next to was concerned about what she heard regarding my trip to Georgia. I couldn't believe it. That bitch dimed me out. She clearly wasn't Italian.

I immediately went into defense mode. Although they'd caught me, I started acting like they weren't going to take me alive. I wasn't going back to Arizona. I had finally escaped, and I wasn't going to let anyone take that away from me.

The officers took my threat and willingness to fight to the death seriously and said that they would need to speak to my mother before any decision was made.

A few minutes later, they came back in the room and informed me that they were putting me on the next flight out to Tucson. I held my ground, explaining to them that I was not getting on that plane. I told them that my stepfather was a very large man who hated me, and if they sent me back, I would certainly have to suffer the consequences of running away.

Tears filled my eyes. I couldn't go back there. I explained that to them. They saw how serious I was. I'm also sure that they didn't want to have to stand toe to toe with a sixteen-year-old kid and physically put him on a plane. That couldn't be good for their image. They immediately got on the phone with my mother and explained the situation to her and then came back to me offering a plea bargain.

They told me that since my mother had legal custody of me (something my father didn't have) they were forced to send me back to her until I could explain to a judge that I was of legal age to decide that I wanted to be with my father. As a compromise, my mother had told the officers that she would pick me up from the airport by herself, and we would have time to talk about it away from my stepfather.

After careful consideration and the realization that this was a situation that I couldn't win at that time, I reluctantly agreed. I was going back to Arizona.

52

WHAT A BEAUTIFUL SURPRISE

I 've had time in my life to ride that plane ride from Arizona to Las Vegas and back many times both on business as well as for pleasure, and I can tell you that no matter what direction you're heading, you are always excited to get off the plane. Regardless of the reason you went to Las Vegas, you always have an opportunity to let loose and do things that you would normally not do in your home town, so on the way there, you can't wait to get off the plane. On the ride home from Vegas, you're usually wiped out from a long trip (too much drinking, etc.) and *can't wait* to get off that plane, get home, and crawl in bed for a week. This happened to be a short plane ride that I wished never ended. I wanted to live on it. I had everything I needed. I had soda, water, pretzels, and a bathroom. Is there anything more precious in life than these?

Against my young adolescent wishes, the plane landed safely at the Tucson freakin' Arizona Airport.

Now, back in the day, family and friends used to be allowed to wait for you at your gate. This was how it was then. I walked as slow as I could through that tunnel of hell waiting to see my mother's face of shame and disappointment. I refused to just walk fast and rip the Band-Aid off. I also half expected to see my stepfather there waiting for me at the gate as well.

When I walked out, my eyes locked with my mother's, and after noticing that my stepfather wasn't there, I immediately put my head down. I wasn't ashamed for what I had done; I was just embarrassed that I had gotten caught … again. I hated myself for telling someone where I was going.

I don't remember her saying anything to me. I don't remember a hug. I don't remember an angry word or even a kind one. That's not to say that none of that happened, but if it did, I can't remember.

Aside from the backpack I was wearing, the suitcase that I'd brought with me was on its way to Georgia, and I immediately wondered why I hadn't just climbed into it instead of chancing anything. I felt a smile start to form as I thought about my luggage reaching my goal without me and vowed that if the only way I was going to get out of Arizona was piece by piece, then so be it.

The three of us walked through the airport without saying a word—just me, my mother and my backpack. I started to grow anxious and a little annoyed with the lack of conversation from a woman who had just received a phone call from the airport police saying that her son was no longer at home, but instead in a different state. One would think that a mother would be chatting up a storm. Something was up, but I just couldn't place what it was.

My suspicions would prove to be valid when we got to the garage and located our vehicle. As we got closer, I noticed that there wasn't anyone in it. My heart rate started to slow down until I saw someone come out from the front of the vehicle where he was hiding.

It was my stepfather.

The ride home was awkward. He didn't say much to me. Or maybe, subconsciously, I blocked out the words while they were being delivered so as not to have to ever relive them. Regardless, I'm sure the way my stepfather "Ninja-Crawled" out from the front of the vehicle was his punishment to me.

There are so many benefits to writing about a life that has been filled with mistakes and remorse. If written properly, the author has the opportunity, maybe even the responsibility to reach out to parents/stepparents/guardians and try to teach them through lessons that there's a possibility that the kids they were in control of can take things you say and do differently than you ever intended them to be delivered.

My stepfather didn't scare me with what he had done that day. What he did do was start to take away some of the respect that I'd had for him.

I've proven in my life that when I'm backed into a corner or someone is overly trying to intimidate me, I become angry and vengeful.

Parents, in some instances, lessons that are to be taught in the style of tough love and/or intimidation aren't always the best policy, because one day your kid will be stronger and faster than you. Just remember that.

53

What Goes Around Comes Around

We got home, and shortly after arriving, my mother made me call my father, who had already been notified of what I had done. His voice over the phone was refreshing. He was sad that I wasn't next to him, but relieved that I was okay. He told me to give him a call tomorrow and let him know how everything was going. Tears welled up in my eyes as I said goodbye to him. I went to bed that night knowing that I would have to face the music tomorrow, but I no longer cared. They couldn't possibly take away anything from me that wasn't already gone.

The next day, a meeting took place with my mother, stepfather, and myself. They told me what my punishment was (which I don't remember) and explained to me very carefully that I would not be allowed to go live with my father. Their threats went in one ear and out the other. To this day, I don't understand what it was that gave them such strong convictions in keeping me in Arizona. I didn't care. I had been caught again and the shame was almost unbearable, but that didn't mean that I was staying. I wanted to see them try to stop me. I had made a promise to myself at one point to leave Arizona without looking back, and I was sticking to that. Eventually, they would have to go to sleep, or work, or the bathroom, or the grocery store. I no longer had the money to hop on a flight, but if I had to crawl on my hands and knees, that's what I was going to do.

A couple days later during an argument with my stepfather in my bedroom, it turned from a verbal altercation to a physical one. Although I remember the details of the fight, I will not put it in this book, because it doesn't really matter at this point. All I knew was that it gave me a reason to come up with another plan.

That Sunday during CCD, (Church school) I snuck off and called my father from a pay phone and told him what had happened. His words were, "Can you get to the airport again?"

I said yes. He then told me that there would be a plane ticket waiting for me and I was not to speak to anyone until we saw each other.

I made arrangements to once again get a ride to the airport, but I couldn't just leave. There had been too many words said and things done to put me in a state of vengeance. I had to leave knowing that I'd had the last word. I looked around the house to see what I could do. I looked to see what kind of damage I could cause, and I continued looking until my eyes rested upon my stepfather's beloved computer. I turned it on and navigated to the DOS operating system, and as soon as it pulled up, I typed in, "Erase DOS," and when prompted to confirm command, I hit Y. It was done.

When it was time, I left that house, walked to the agreed-upon rendezvous point and left for the airport. Forty-five minutes later, I walked in, got my ticket, went through security, waited for the plane to board, and then boarded it. I was now on a one-way direct flight out of there. I pulled down the shade next to me, and as the plane started down the runway, I closed my eyes and smiled. I was leaving Arizona. And I wasn't looking back.

PART 4

54

GREENER GRASS

I didn't dream of anything in particular during that plane ride. At least I don't remember dreaming about anything, but what I do remember was opening my eyes for the first time to see a semiattractive flight attendant leaning over me and welcoming me to Atlanta, Georgia. She had a very pleasant and sincere smile, and I couldn't help but to smile back.

I leaned up in my chair and it hit me. I had made it. I was out of Arizona and free from a life I didn't want. My hands started to sweat and goose bumps formed on my skin. I was nervous, but very excited to see my father.

I stepped off the plane and through the tunnel. When I came out at the other end, my father was standing there with my uncle. It felt like it had been a life time since I saw my father. His eyes started to well up and my eyes followed suit. We hugged and my new life began.

We hurried out of that airport, and I kept finding myself looking behind me. I felt that at any moment the parental units of Arizona were sure to jump out from behind something and take me back to hell. I wasn't going this time. I would fight no matter what. I was home, and that was all that mattered.

We escaped the airport without incident, found our car in the parking area, and took off toward home. The car ride flew by with excited and nervous conversation from both my father and me. I think we were both shocked that I was in Georgia.

My father handed me some cash and told me to hide it in my wallet and never spend it. He told me that if something should happen, I was to run as fast as I could and use the money to stay away until we could meet up again. I remember taking the money; the feel of it was different. Up until now, I didn't realize why it felt foreign to me. It wasn't just money to me. It was the reason to stay with my father. It was reassurance. I was with a man whom I had always wanted to live with. I was with a person who believed in me. My mother believed in me in her way, but the huge defining difference was that when I would visit my father every weekend when I was young, before Arizona, he'd showed me, without fail, that there was love. There was support and an environment that *showcased* unconditional love.

When we got in view of my father's house, a warm feeling came over me. There wouldn't be any more running. I wouldn't have to look into bus tickets and plane tickets. I could settle in, plant my feet, and build a life. My father pulled into the garage, and we walked upstairs to the kitchen area where there was a large Welcome Home sign and my stepmother's smiling face. Seeing that sign is one of the happiest memories I have.

55

LADIES AND GENTLEMAN OF THE JURY

My mother received the phone call sometime that morning to say that I had arrived safely in Georgia. I don't know how the conversation went with her and my father, but I'm assuming that it didn't go very well, because when my father got off the phone with her, he was making preparations to set up a meeting with an attorney. He was keeping his word, he was going to fight for me. Nothing was going to take his kid away from him again.

The next day, my father, stepmother, and I met with the attorney. From what I gathered, my mother was pissed that I was there and said that she would not relinquish custody to my father. She would not sign over rights. I didn't understand what the big deal was and became quite annoyed with the whole process. I was of legal age to decide where I wanted to be, and had gone through some extreme situations to prove that I was not happy in Arizona and wanted to be with my father in Georgia.

The attorney was very professional as he sat there and listened to my father summarize what the situation looked like and what he would like to see happen. The attorney then turned to me and asked for my side of the story. I told him everything, including the details of the scuffle between my stepfather and me. With that, he saw his opportunity. He would use the fight story as leverage, because my stepfather was a cop and that story would just cause too much unwanted attention.

It was a great plan that for some reason I felt guilty for. My stepfather wasn't a bad man back then. He's not a bad man today, and I'm guessing he won't be a bad man tomorrow. He was disciplining a kid the best way he knew how. I never held that against him. I feel, even to this day, that discipline is an essential form of parenting. However, you have to make sure that the kid you are disciplining is actually your kid. Just sayin'.

Through the next couple of days, there were many conversations between my mother and father. This was a situation that required a lot of attention because attorneys aren't cheap when you live in the same area, but imagine the cost of a custody battle from across the country! No one wanted that, and eventually my mother conceded. She would agree to let me live with my father, but with a stipulation. She would not sign over full custody to my father, but would consent to allowing the move to happen. I never learned what my mother's true reasoning for putting up such a fight in letting me live with my father, nor do I care. If I had to guess, I would say that she was just trying to protect me from the common childhood mistake of running away from my problems. Regardless, the consent she gave was enough to get me enrolled in school. I was staying, and to top it off, I was going to be a Sprayberry High School Yellow Jacket!

I was so excited. I can look back on it now and laugh. I believe in signs, and I should have listened to this one that was just screaming out at me. I had finally arrived at a destination I wanted to be at for so long, only to attend a high school that had a bee as a mascot. Of all things, a bee! The one thing I'm allergic to! On a side note, let me just say, that the person who edited this book, wrote that a yellow jacket is actually a wasp. My message to the editor, "Look buddy, if something stabs you with it's 'ass'knive,' it's a freakin' bee."

56

Back to School

My father went with me to enroll in the school, and it was an experience I will never forget. While we were walking through the halls that day, we passed a gentleman who claimed to be the vice-principal. His name for all intents and purposes is going to be Mr. Bumnuts. I can tell you that right off the bat I didn't like this guy. He just had a way about him. I don't know if it was the way he smirked or the way he carried himself, but if I were a betting man, I'd put my money on the probability that he was someone who got picked on at school and finally found revenge by going back as an authority figure. I knew I was in trouble. Hell, I remember wanting to punch him in his smug nose right then and there.

My father's house was within walking distance to the school, but other than that, I don't remember anything about my first day. That's really weird for me, because even though I had a lot of first days of school, I can remember pretty much all of them.

I do remember the classes were pretty tough, and I didn't really fit in that well. One of my friends from Arizona had told me that I would totally fit in because I was dressing like a cowboy and Georgia is predominately a hick-friendly state. I didn't see that as I looked around though. It was more alternative than country.

One day in class I heard a girl snickering behind me. I turned around to see some slim blonde girl trying to quickly cover up her laugh. I smiled at her initially thinking that maybe she had a little crush on me. After all, why wouldn't she? I turned back around starting to think about our first date. Do Georgia girls like to do different things? I started to plan for it. I would need to ask my father for some money and then secure a ride. Maybe she would want to see a movie? I made a mental note to check the show times and listings as soon as I got home. Then there was the issue of wardrobe selection. Should I wear the Wranglers with the white T-shirt, or should I really get dressed up and wear the Wranglers with the black T-shirt?

She giggled again, and I knew I was in trouble. This girl was totally into me, and I didn't have a solid plan on where I was going to take her. I tried to close my eyes and get my mind back to paying attention to what the teacher was teaching, but then realized it's hard to pay attention in class with your eyes closed.

My mind wandered to a field filled with a beautiful array of blue, red, yellow and purple flowers. We were hand in hand, skipping. Butterflies flitted around us. We were happy and in love.

My fantasy came to a screeching halt when I felt a tap on my shoulder. This was it. She wanted to talk to me. She was so obsessed with me that I was sure she was going to ask *me* out and I wouldn't have to stress about asking her and then planning it.

I turned around and our eyes met. She was more beautiful than I remembered from minutes before. I smiled like a true Italian country boy and said, "Hey, how are you?" in my new Georgia country accent.

She said, "Have you ever seen that movie, *Toy Story?*

"Yeah ..." I replied

She laughed and asked me for my autograph. I didn't understand what she was talking about so I smiled and said, "Huh, what do you mean?" Any moment she was going to tell me that she was sorry. She was just really nervous and couldn't think of how to ask me out. I felt bad for her.

After many giggles from her and now the girls around her, she told me that she wanted my autograph because I looked just like, "Woody" from the movie—the scrawny cowboy toy doll.

The room erupted with laughter. I looked her straight in the eyes, ready to explode, and said, "Excuse me," walked out of the classroom, the building, and down the road. I was taking the rest of the day off.

57

TIME TO WRESTLE

I decided to give wrestling another shot. After all, I was living with my father, and he loved wrestling; he was, in fact, the reason I'd done it in Arizona. I was constantly looking for approval from him—and pretty much everyone I looked up to in one way or another.

It wasn't an easy process. The level of wrestling in Georgia was at a level I couldn't believe. By the time the kids got to high school, they were seasoned veterans. They started kids wrestling out there in grammar school! It seems these kids were born wearing headgear and a singlet. I was in way over my head, but I couldn't just *not* do it. I wanted to impress my father, so I was going to throw everything I had into it.

Our coach was a young guy with ridiculous wrestling abilities! I was shocked, because in the hallway, he looked like the kind of guy you'd want to give a wedgie and then throw into a locker. Of course, that would have been a mistake.

Practice started out pretty exciting for me, because the mat we practiced on was a donated authentic mat from the summer Olympics, which had taken place in Georgia that year. I was practicing on a piece of American history. I felt blessed, and it made me want to try harder.

A few weeks into practice it was time to *wrestle off.* In case you don't know, a wrestle-off is a team's internal contest to make the cut for a match. Being on the wrestling team is not something that's just given to you. Every week before a match, the wrestlers in your weight class would have to wrestle each other for a spot on varsity or junior varsity. You could be on the team one week and a defeated, distant memory the next. I was going to make the team. I thought I had to: my father's feelings about me would change if I didn't.

There were three kids in my weight class and only two spots to grab. Of course, luck having it, my first match would be against the guy who had been wrestling since he was a little kid. I wish I could say I was putting on a good show, but I wasn't. I was being out-matched, and to top it off, Mr. Bumnuts was there. I had noticed, in between exhausting periods, that he was whispering to the guy next to him; I could have sworn I caught him smiling at me a few times, as if to taunt me. I brushed it off. It was too horrible. I needed to clear my head. I needed to concentrate to get out of this alive.

This was my second official year of wrestling, and although I felt that I was highly talented, the incredible hulk that was in front of me was determined to prove me wrong. I lasted the entire match without getting pinned, but lost badly in points. If I was smart about it, I would have let him pin me, because I still had to wrestle again for a spot on the JV team, but my pride wouldn't let me. I was completely out of energy.

I was banking on the next match going a little easier. My opponent wasn't as seasoned as the Olympic champion I had just faced. I was tired, and I knew I wouldn't be able to go the distance again, so if there was an opportunity to get rid of this kid, I would need to take advantage of it. Right out of the gate, the other guy, obviously nervous, shot in on my legs. I saw it coming a mile away and sprawled, cross-facing the hell out of him. I threw him on his back and pinned him. I did it! Even though it was only junior varsity, I had made the team. An overwhelming feeling of stress was leaving my body. Now I could go home and tell my father that I had tried my hardest, but it would be JV for now.

When my father got home from work, I delivered the news. I wasn't sure how he was going to take it, because it wasn't varsity. But he smiled and congratulated me. He was genuinely proud and excited for me. I couldn't stop smiling. I had done well.

That night, we had a really nice dinner. I don't remember what I ate; I just know that I was really hungry. The next morning would be weigh-ins, but that didn't concern me because after all, how much weight can you gain from eating some supper?

58

MATCH OR MISS

The next morning, I woke up even earlier than normal. I was extremely excited about what was happening in my life. I had not only made *a* wrestling team, but I did it in Georgia against all talent and odds. To make things better, my father was going to come to the match and see his son wrestle for the first time.

After breakfast, I grabbed my things for school and started walking. I had more pep in my step that morning. If this was still the '80s, I'd have been dancing my way to school while singing along to the song "Walking On Sunshine" blaring from invisible speakers in the sky. Life was great, and nothing was going to get me down—even the thought of the *Toy Story* girl didn't bother me anymore. Besides, I was going to be an amazing wrestler, and she would soon be chasing me yelling, "Please, Woody, give me another chance, I'm a dumbass!"

When I arrived at the school, I went straight downstairs to the wrestling room. A lot of the wrestlers were already there, and I started to get a little anxious. It was different when my mother had come to a couple of my matches, or my brother saw me win one and dramatically point to him as if to thank him for all he had done for me. This was my father. This was a different game.

I waited nervously in line to be weighed. I wasn't nervous about wrestling, per se, but there's just something about lines that make me anxious. It could either be a line where you're physically standing there, or an alphabetical line where you know when your name is going to be called, but you still have to wait. Doesn't matter. Lines scare the shit out of me.

At one point while in line, I looked up to see that my best friend, the vice- principal, was monitoring the weigh-ins. Awesome. I couldn't wait to get up there in my undies and stand in front of a man who I couldn't quite figure out why I hated.

When it was my turn to step on the scale, Mr. Bumnuts made a motion with his head to the official weigh-in guy, and the next thing I knew, I was going to be weighed in by my arch nemesis. I stared at him for a few seconds, and I thought I could faintly hear the whistling sound from the old Wild West movies when two men stood across from each other at high noon. I imagined a tumbleweed rolling across the dirty road as Bumnuts and I were about to draw our guns. I knew when the smoke cleared that I was going to be standing and he was not.

Then I heard an impatient, "Jason, let's go," and just like that, the gunfight was over. It was time to officially step on the scale. I laughed to myself as my naked feet stepped on that scale. What a great fantasy I'd just had. It was a little morbid, but nonetheless pretty funny.

I was watching as he adjusted the sliders to find my correct weight. 100, 120, 130, 132, 135, 137 … 137?… *137!*

I couldn't believe it! Somehow, someway, I had mysteriously gained seven pounds overnight, and I was now over my weight limit! I looked up at him and said that there must be some kind of mistake. He said, "Nope, the scale doesn't lie. I guess you'll need to try and cut the weight in the next hour, or you'll forfeit your position to wrestle for this school this time."

I was pissed! There was no freakin' way this was happening to me. It HAD to be him! Somehow, he'd tampered with the scale. There was no way I gained that much weight overnight.

I didn't have time to argue. This asshole wasn't going to beat me. I wasn't going to lose because Bumnuts had some sick and twisted vendetta against me.

I ran to the storage closet and threw on as many clothes as I could. Then I went into my backpack and grabbed my CD Walkman, opened it up, and put in the *Rocky IV* soundtrack. I turned up the volume and started running. I had to sweat off a lot of weight. I tried to get myself lost in the words of the soundtrack, as if Sylvester Stallone was going to be my Tony Robbins and, through positive thinking, the weight would just come right off. With every song, I ran faster. With every motivational beat, I ran harder. When my legs couldn't take anymore abuse, I mentally yelled at them to *Man Up!"* and stopped just long enough to grab a jump rope and torture them some more.

Before long, my time was up, and I needed to weigh in again. With all the strength I had left, I removed my clothing including my undies, and once again stood in front of Mr. Bumnuts. This time, with my own nuts in hand.

He moved the slides over again. My heart sank when they rested on a number that was still two pounds outside of my weight class. I didn't have any more time. He had won.

I got dressed and left the wrestling room as fast as I could. By now, school had officially started, and I was late for class. I walked into first-period history, my face completely red with embarrassment, frustration, and defeat. I thought that if I could just get through this class, I would be able to calm down a little. The students looked at me as I walked to my desk, and I could feel a volcano deep in my stomach start to explode as I sensed their eyes on me.

With the fury of ten men, I threw my backpack against the wall, yelled as loud as I could and walked out. I needed to get away. Screw Georgia. Screw the wrestling team. Screw the high school, and screw Bumnuts! I walked into the bathroom, locked myself in a stall, sat down, and started to cry.

A few minutes later, a kid from my wrestling team who was also in my history class came in and asked if I was okay. I said yes, and he told me that he explained everything to the teacher, and I shouldn't feel embarrassed. He said that it took a lot of heart to try to cut that much weight that fast. He told me I had nothing to be ashamed of, and next week I would make the team again, and all would be fine.

I thanked him, walked out of the stall, splashed water on my face and then went for a walk.

I needed to find a payphone. I needed to call my father.

When the phone started ringing, I started to feel sick to my stomach. My father's calm voice came on the line. I immediately busted out with more tears as, defeated, I told my father that I didn't make weight and he wouldn't be able to see me wrestle. He said it was okay and tried to calm me down. I was clearly more upset about him not seeing me wrestle than he was. We got off the phone, and I went back to class. I knew I wouldn't be able to concentrate the rest of the day, so I just sat there class after class, staring at the wall until the bell rang.

I was no longer on the wrestling team. I was no longer excited about the new school. Something had changed in me. I wasn't happy anymore.

59

WHY WOULD THAT EVER HAPPEN?

I went to the wrestling match anyways because I wanted to support the team, but also to see what the guy I was supposed to wrestle looked like.

My JV replacement got up to wrestle in my spot and had his opponent (my opponent) pinned in the first minute of the first period. WTF? That should have been me.

That night, my father did his best to cheer me up, and I did my best to convince him that I was okay. I wasn't though. I didn't understand what was wrong with me, and once again I had questions. How could something as stupid as not being able to wrestle change my whole mental concept? How could something that stupid try to convince me that everything I had done to get there didn't matter anymore and make me ready to leave. Where was I planning on going? How was I going to get there? More importantly, how could I stop feeling this way?

I lay in bed that night unable to sleep. There were so many questions, and I knew that even if I searched really hard for the answers, I wouldn't be able to find them.

I woke up the next day and decided to try to put everything behind me. After all, I had been through worse than what was going on right now, and I needed to concentrate and do the right thing.

I started to walk to school that morning, and I felt I had a new-found desire to become a scholar. I wanted to succeed. All the horrible feelings from the day before vanished, just like that! If I'd been more aware of the wonderful world of psychology, I would have asked myself how this could be, but I just figured that I was thinking more positively now, and that was normal. Right?

When I arrived at the school, I walked through the halls like I was ready for anything. I looked around and everyone was oddly quiet. No one was saying much, a lot of people were crying and everyone was moving very slowly. There was a very creepy feeling in the air. It was unsettling. I couldn't allow this feeling to take over my new, positive thinking, so just when I was about to yell, "Hey, what's going on? I feel like I'm at a freakin' funeral," two emotional girls passed me and one said to the other, "I can't believe they're dead."

I bit my lip right away and stopped in my steps. Did I just hear her correctly? Did she just say that? My eyes stopped working; I couldn't see clearly. I started to shake. Someone was dead, and I didn't know who. I didn't know how. I was helpless. I needed to find out. As the next person passed me, I reached out and grabbed his arm to stop him and get some answers. I looked over to see that the arm I grabbed belonged to Mr. Bumnuts. Great!

He pulled his arm away and seemed very angry with what I had just done to him. He asked me what I thought I was doing. I told him that I was sorry for grabbing his arm, but I wanted to know what was going on. He said he couldn't talk about it right now and stormed off like a Grammy award winning diva. Jerk.

I walked to my locker and listened to the tearful accounts of what had taken place the night before. The story I got was that three of the varsity cheerleaders went to throw toilet paper on the house of the freshman cheerleader as a form of initiation. As they were TP'ing the house, the freshman cheerleader's father came out and caught the girls vandalizing his property. Instead of just scaring them away, he decided to hop in his car and speed off down the road after them. As the three varsity girls tried to take a corner, they lost control of the vehicle and flipped it. All three girls were killed. I was in classes with these girls. I, at one point, sat next to them. I was shocked. The school was shocked.

How could a man do that? It was only toilet paper. It was only a joke, and now three girls were gone.

I went to wrestling practice after school that day, but the team was in a weird mood, and no one was really up for practicing when three of our classmates had just died. We called off the rest of practice, and I walked home. When I got there, my stepmother asked me if I knew any of the girls, and I said not really and acted like it didn't bother me, but it did.What did these three girls do to deserve this? I started to lose the new faith I had just found. That faith would be a constantly fleeing part of my life from then on.

60

DISAPPOINTING

Considering that I don't have a long and distinguishing wrestling career to speak about, I'm going to summarize the rest of my wrestling experience now, so we can lay this topic to rest.

I started to date a girl over that last month of wrestling. and I know without a doubt that was taking a lot of my focus off of wrestling. Because I was a sixteen-year-old boy and girls were something that just appealed to me, I was skipping some practices here and there to hang out with her after school. I couldn't help it. I was getting to experience a side of life that I had only witnessed on late-night Cinemax. But I couldn't miss too many practices, or I would be ineligible to wrestle off for a spot in my weight class that next week.

When it was time to win a spot on the team that next week, I showed up ready to take on the guy that had beaten me for the varsity spot the time before. This time it was a little bit different because I got to watch the kid I'd beaten the week before wrestle our Varsity Star. This was pretty exciting for me, because after all, I'd kicked that kid's ass when I was tired, so wrestling him after *he's* tired would be a cakewalk. I saw him get thrown around and lose the first match, and after he regained some composure, he was going to face me.

I stepped on the mat and looked at this kid who was still breathing a little heavy and actually felt bad for him. He looked pitiful, but this was wrestling, and I wasn't going to go soft on him. I was going to come out and destroy this puny person.

When the whistle blew, I went after him like a horny fat kid at a brothel buffet. My attack was relentless. Unfortunately, his defense was better, and before I knew it, I was on my back and in serious trouble. He was winning! I had to do something. This wasn't happening. I sprawled to avoid the pin and got out of it. We got back to our feet, and I stood there breathing heavy, in disbelief. Stepping back a few feet, I tried to regain composure, and after a few seconds, I convinced myself that every dog has his day and what had just happened to this future All-American was a fluke.

Shaking it off, I stepped forward, and we locked arms. I started to force him backward, and I knew that I owned him. I felt my strength coming back to me and my confidence return. I was about to flip this kid over and send him packing when the darnedest thing happened—he flipped me over, pinned me, and sent *me* packing. What the hell?

I couldn't believe what had just happened to me. I'd lost! And he wasn't even good. I grabbed my stuff, changed in the locker room, and started walking home. How was I going to tell my father? He was sure to not like the news.

I imagined myself standing in front of an old-school, English judge, the one with the big white wig—you know the kind. Except this judge was not English; he was my father.

I would stand there shaking as he said, "Jason Ventre, you are being charged with being cocky, conceited, and lazy. How do you plea?"

I would whisper, "Innocent?"

The judge would point his gavel at me and yell, "Silence!" and then sentence me to "Life … in Arizona!"

I knew I was being silly, but I couldn't help it. I didn't lose to Mr. Junior Varsity, I lost to myself. Who the hell did I think I was walking into that match like I was God's gift to the singlet?

When my father got home, he gave me a hug and immediately asked me how the matches went. He was anxious to hear if I'd made the varsity team this time. I put my head down and said no. He said, "That's okay," and that things take time and junior varsity will do. I weakly told him that I hadn't made that either, and I felt the hesitation in his voice when he said, "Oh, well … you'll get it next time."

I knew without a doubt that my father was trying to be supportive, but still was disappointed. What good came out of the whole situation was when I told him how I had lost, it sparked this feeling in him to want to help his son. We went outside and practiced together. He had quite a bit of knowledge, and every day up until the next time I tried for the team; we were outside rolling around working on my moves. I had never had that type of relationship with anyone. It was the quintessential *baseball-toss-in-the-backyard* kind of relationship. It was amazing.

When it was time to wrestle off again, I was ready. This time, it was from a position of preparedness, not conceit. My first match that day was with my junior varsity buddy, and when I stepped on that mat, I felt different. I felt like my father was in there with me.

At the sound of the whistle, I attacked with controlled chaos and muscled my way past my opponent onto victory via a pin in the second period.

I was pumped. I was reenergized, but focused on my next opponent. If I could find a way to beat Hercules, I would make varsity! I did understand that it was a long shot, but I would try my best. When it was time to wrestle, we received word that he was unable to wrestle off this week; the winner of the last match would be automatically given the title of varsity wrestler! I couldn't believe it! I know I hadn't earned it, but a win is a win, and I started fantasizing about giving my father the big news.

My excitement was cut short when Mr. Bumnuts entered and said that he couldn't allow me to wrestle on the varsity team. I stood there shocked. This guy was a short and curly away from getting his first student-induced concussion.

The coach asked why, and Bumnuts explained that because my mother had only given permission for me to *live* with my father, it wasn't full custody. Because of this, the rule was that junior varsity was as far as I was allowed to compete at. I never challenged Bumnuts interpretation of Georgia High School law. I didn't think of a reason why someone in his position would lie about that. Hmm.

Words can't describe how upset I was.

I left practice and went home to deliver the news to my father. He once again was optimistic about the whole thing and promised that these things had a way of working themselves out. He then asked what time the match was. I told him, ate a *small* dinner, and went to sleep. Weigh-ins were the next morning, and I needed my strength in case Bumnuts was there telling me that I had gained a hundred pounds overnight.

When I got to school, I walked down to the wrestling room and prepared to step on the scale once again. I was relieved to see that Bumnuts must have slept in, because he was nowhere to be seen. To make sure that he wouldn't just Houdini his way into the room to vandalize my chances of wrestling again, I pushed myself through the line and practically hopscotched my way onto the scale. I had made weight, and I was relieved. I needed to call my father and tell him the good news.

When I dialed the number, I was met with his usual upbeat voice, and I told him that I'd made weight. He congratulated me, but said that he just found out he wouldn't be able to go to my match because of work. I almost dropped the phone. My world started to cave in again. Tears started to form, and I wanted to hang up the phone. I cleared my throat and told him that it was okay and that there would be plenty of matches in the future. He told me that he would see if he could get Uncle Jerry to go in his place. I thanked him, and we hung up the phone.

I spent the rest of the day unable to pay attention in class. I liked Uncle Jerry, but he wasn't my father. I wouldn't have the same feeling about him witnessing me wrestle.

I had no choice; these were the cards I was dealt, and I just had to live with them.

With Uncle Jerry visible in the stands, I felt a little better than what I'd felt when I first heard the news, but I still couldn't shake the reminder that my father wasn't there.

When my name was called, I put on my headgear, gave one last look up to Uncle Jerry, and stepped onto the mat.

When the whistle blew, I immediately saw an opening where I could shoot in on my opponent's legs and take him down. But I shot in off-balance and sloppy, and he picked up on it, flipped me over, and in the time it took for Uncle Jerry to open his car door and get inside to come see me wrestle, this guy beat me. I was so embarrassed.

I'm sure that Uncle Jerry tried to make me feel better that day, but I don't remember it. My mind was blank. It had dawned on me that I was an absolutely incredible wrestler in my head, where it doesn't count. I guess I just assumed that because my father did well in the sport, I would. Well, let me tell you, it doesn't work that way.

Over the next couple of weeks, I would attend less and less practice and spend more time hanging out and doing anything I could to not have to practice. I had quit the team, and I never wanted to go back.

One day my father came home from work early and saw me sitting on the couch eating chips and watching TV. He said hello and then asked why I wasn't at wrestling practice. I told him that I couldn't wrestle anymore because I was failing all my classes, and if I didn't pick them up, I may not graduate on time.

It was a weak excuse, but I couldn't tell him that I didn't have the heart to wrestle. He said, "Okay, that's too bad, but your school work is very important." I thought I did a great job selling my bullshit lie to him, but the reality was that he did a great job of selling me on the idea that he believed what I was saying.

Things would only go downhill from there.

61

STICKY FINGERS

With wrestling behind me and my grades continuing to travel in the wrong direction, I started to feel a little cornered. I'm not the type of person to want to excel when the pressure is on. When I do something good, it's because I decided to, not because my back is against the wall and people expect good things from me. I'm just odd like that.

The classes that I was taking were really challenging. I was in one class studying rocks. Now, there's actually a scientific name for it, but as you can imagine, if I don't even know what the name of the class was, I was probably not doing that great in it. Besides, who the hell wants to make a career out of studying rocks? I didn't see a point. I had only chosen the class because of the person who invented the Pet Rock back in the '70s. I figured we would learn about him and study his success. Oh no, I wasn't that lucky! We were studying volcanos and mountains and shit. I hated it.

I started to put up a wall around myself and anything close to me. School. Family. Sports. I hated being in that building. It was like a constant reminder that I had failed. What was I doing in Georgia? My whole point was to be with my father, and I guess, through that experience, become close to him and gain that acceptance that I still, to this day, look for. Unfortunately, I started lying to him about how I was doing in school. I felt bad for telling him that I'd quit the team because of my grades, but then didn't work to raise them, so I just told him that I was doing better than when I was on the team.

I *can* tell you from experience that once you start to lie to someone you care about, it's all downhill from there. The problem with lying to a loved one is that you have to keep lying. If you lie to strangers and the situation becomes a little uncomfortable, you can just throw your hands up and say that you lied because you really don't give a shit about them. But when you lie to someone you care about, you have to have another lie handy to back up the first one. It's a never-ending cycle.

Well, I can honestly tell you I had become that person. I had become a liar.

To make matters worse, my father and stepmother had given me so much trust that they would brag about me to their neighbors, and the neighbors would eventually start asking me to babysit. At that time in my life, that probably wasn't the best decision.

While the kids were asleep, I would walk around the house and look at and take what they had. At first it started happening just because I was bored and there was nothing on TV; then it turned into an obsession. I felt like a cat burglar who had just snuck into someone's house—I was looking for anything valuable.

I wasn't stealing money, because that would imply that I was a smart thief. No, not me, I would take stupid things that had no real cash relevance. I would take baseball cards; lighters; cheap, fake jewelry. I had become a freakin' kleptomaniac!

One night, I was babysitting one of the neighbors' kids, and after he had gone to sleep, I put on my imaginary ski mask and grabbed the flashlight that didn't exist and went scavenging for some treasure. I got to the basement, which I never really went into because it was kind of creepy. Can you imagine? I was a thief that was afraid of the dark.

After looking through some boxes for a while, I came across the mother lode! There, before me was a collection of dirty magazines the world has never seen! There were *thousands and thousands* of nasty mags just staring up at me as if to say, "Come on, Jase, you know you want us."

I did want them; I totally wanted them. What sixteen-year-old kid wouldn't? I put down the Faberge egg I was holding and grabbed some bathroom reading.[10]

I flipped through the pages, not stopping to read the articles and KNEW that I needed to have these. I called one of my friends on the phone and explained the situation. Without hesitating, he hopped into his car and cruised on over. When his eyes rested upon the holy grail of adult reading, he stopped in his tracks, and for a few seconds was unable to breath. We knew what we wanted to do. We were going to somehow extract the goods from the building and try to sell them on the streets to other kids our age who would stand to gain a lot from this type of education. Why can't they teach *porn* in school? Call me crazy, but I think kids would be a lot happier there if that were the case.

After many teenage minutes of pondering our next move, we started the extraction. We took hundreds and hundreds of magazines out of that house and buried them in the woods behind my parents' house. Now I can honestly tell you that, to this day, I don't really understand why the hell anyone would bury dirty magazines. They weren't bones, and I wasn't a dog. I guess I just

---

[10] Okay, you know I'm just kidding; I wasn't really holding a Faberge egg.

figured that the ground would be the last place anyone would go searching for something of that nature.

I wish I could tell you that our adult magazine business netted us an immense fortune, but I can't. We ended up selling a couple of them to some fourteen-year-old kid who had just learned that calcium isn't the only good thing about a boob. We eventually stopped caring about the business and would close the doors to our entrepreneurial existence and completely forget about the immense amount of magazines buried in the ground.

One night I was in my room, and I started to think about the things that I was doing. My dream of this amazing life with my father was turning into a nightmare. I went to my secret hiding place in my room.[11] I had somehow amassed quite the collection of items with relatively no value. I had managed to steal a bunch of junk. It was getting hard to hide all these items, and I started to feel an overwhelming amount of pressure. I knew I was going to need to find a way out of this situation, and I needed to find a way out soon before I got caught with all of this stuff.

My beautiful green grass was starting to harden and discolor. The grass was not greener on the other side. In fact, I was the one on the other side, just standing there peeing on the lawn.

---

[11] Parents, I can promise you, *every* kid has one of those at one point or another.)

62

Home Alone

My life was starting to spiral out of control, and I wasn't sure how to handle it. I was no longer with the girl I had hung out with to skip wrestling practice, I was now with a different girl. One day my father asked me if I was okay, and I saw my opportunity. I told him that I wasn't very happy being there and I wasn't sure if Georgia was the place for me. He was shocked. He couldn't believe what he was hearing. I had only been there for around four months or so, and I was just all of a sudden not happy? He didn't understand.

Neither did I.

For as long as I've known my father, he's always been a very level-headed, energetic, lovable guy. At that point in my life, I had never seen him get angry. I hadn't even heard him swear before. This situation was no different. He calmly put his hand on my shoulder, looked me in the eyes, and said that we were going to work through whatever issues I was having: everything was going to be fine.

He told me that he and my stepmother were going to go away for Valentine's Day. It was his gift to her. It was a weekend getaway, and they asked me to take care of the house.

Me? The trust they had for me was unprecedented. To make matters even *more* ridiculous, they had made plans to let their two young sons stay with the neighbors while they were gone, so I had the house COMPLETELY to myself.

The situation grew into the makings of a sitcom. I could just picture Dr. and Mrs. Seaver telling Kirk Cameron that he was going to be home alone and there weren't any parties allowed. Of course they would come home to a wrecked house with empty alcohol bottles everywhere! Fortunately for him, *Growing Pains* was a show and not real life, so he would only be in trouble for a few minutes.

I couldn't let any of that garbage happen. I needed to be good. There hadn't been anyone up until that point who had put that much faith and trust in me. I couldn't betray that. My father asked me for a favor—to not make any decisions to go anywhere until he came back from his trip. He said that we would work everything out then. I said okay and truly intended to be good and wait for that conversation to present itself.

I had decided to live up to my word, to be the son that my father deserved.

The day they left was not as exciting for me as I thought it would be. I believed with my whole heart that I wasn't going to do anything wrong that weekend, but as I watched them get ready to leave, I was already feeling guilty. I didn't know why. Maybe it was because I had been up to no good for so long in my life or maybe I didn't believe myself when I promised myself I wouldn't do anything bad. It was a horrible feeling, and I hated it.

I walked Dad and Bobbie to the garage and gave them both a hug and a kiss and watched as they drove off in my father's car.

I looked around the house and thought to myself, *Hmm, what now?* I knew that the trick to staying out of trouble with that much freedom was to just keep my mind occupied. So as if I were the main character in a video game, I looked over what I had in my inventory. I didn't have much money; I had lost my glasses; and I didn't have a driver's license at all. How much trouble could a kid without those essential trouble-making tools get into?

I spent the next couple of hours doing everything a sixteen-year-old kid should do while his parents were away. I ate as much junk food as I could. Made long-distance phone calls to some friends back in Arizona, and then stripped down to my undies and tried to replay the scene from *Risky Business*, using a wooden spatula as a microphone. When it was very evident that my performance was absolutely amazing, there was only one thing left to do. I put on the *Footloose* soundtrack, stripped off the undies, and streaked around the house, stopping to dance in front of every mirror in my attempt to dance like Kevin Bacon. When that got old, I serenaded myself with R. Kelly's inspiring hit, "I Believe I Can Fly." It was very motivational. By the end of it, I felt that anything was possible. I went to the garage for a quick workout.

After a grueling fifteen-minute workout, I was ready for a nap. I lay on my bed thinking that I was doing a good job, and if I could just get through tonight without incident, I would be in good shape. I closed my eyes and was ready to drift off to the land of responsibility. Ten minutes later, I opened my eyes and realized that there was no way I could sleep.

I grabbed the cordless phone and called the girl I was seeing. As I talked to her on the phone, I walked around my father's house as if it was my own personal mansion. The only thing I was missing was a smoking jacket and some Playboy models. I even spoke more clearly into the phone as I went into the liquor cabinet to show off, asking her what was a good thing to drink. I said okay and started searching for some cognac. Not really knowing what I was looking for, I spotted something green, gave up on the cognac, grabbed the Pucker—some flavored vodka—and took a swig. I thought that it was sweet, but kind of gross. I figured that maybe beer was a better idea.

I went into the refrigerator and pulled out a Samuel Adams. Mimicking my father's love for the beer, I opened it, and took a big gulp. I almost threw up, but instead threw out the beer, and went back for the Pucker.

Thirty minutes later, I found myself standing in front of the mirror staring at myself. I no longer cared about what the girl on the other end was saying. I was mesmerized by my own reflection. The guy I was looking at had a really red face and a look in his eyes that told me, he really didn't give a shit about anything. I was worried about him, because I stood there standing still, but he was swaying back and forth. I laughed at him and figured that he surely needed to get some help, because he might have a drinking problem.

On the other end of the phone, I heard someone say "Hello?" as if she was trying to find out if I had hung up. I told her that I needed to get some sleep, and I would call her tomorrow. She said okay; I hung up the phone, staggered upstairs, and passed out in the hallway five feet from my bedroom door.

I woke up the next morning, and my head was screaming at me. I said "Fucking Pucker" out loud, and then laughed because I thought it rhymed. Picking myself up off the floor, I was concerned when I realized that I was naked and had forgotten how that could have happened. Slowly, it came back to me. I went to my room, grabbed some fresh clothes, and walked downstairs only to find my undies hanging from the pantry door handle. That made me laugh too. I remember thinking that I wished I could have hung out with myself last night—it appeared that I was a lot of fun to be around.

I decided to make myself some breakfast and opened the pantry. I bypassed the Cinnamon Toast Crunch, Captain Crunch, and the other normal breakfast foods. I was an adult now. A real man. A drinking man. I needed something that expressed my new persona.

I grabbed the Chips-Ahoys, the Yodels, and a cupcake. Swinging over to the refrigerator, I topped off the gourmet meal with some milk, and sat down for a feast.

Before I knew it, the cupcake was gone, the Chips-Ahoys were sailing around my stomach, and the Yodels were on board singing. It was the best breakfast ever! I wanted to kiss the chef.

Sitting there made me realize that I couldn't just waste away my day; I needed to come up with a game plan. I grabbed a piece of paper and wrote down an itinerary:

9:00 a.m.—Breakfast ✓
9:30—Bathroom
9:40—Shower
10:00—Video games
Noon—Lunch
12:30—Video games
1:00—Call the girl
1:30—Video games
5:00—Dinner
5:30—Video games
11:00—Call the girl
11:30—Bedtime

I had made my list and looked it over. I felt proud and grown up. I had a schedule, and I needed to get to it. This was a schedule that was sure to keep me out of trouble. I had a lot of work to do, and I needed to get to it so I could accomplish all that I had set out to do.

Sticking to the schedule proved to be very easy for me. I had eaten breakfast; then I spent time in the bathroom, played my video games, ate lunch, played more games, called the girl, went back to the video games, and then ate dinner. I was really tired, but I still had things that needed to get done and had managed not to do anything completely stupid thus far. I was actually keeping my promise!

After dinner, I naturally went back to checking things off the list, and after four and a half hours, mastered the Nintendo game Aladdin. I played that game so long that I felt really close to the main character, as if we were best friends or something. I called the girl, looking forward to getting the conversation over so I could hop into bed. My eyes were exhausted from focusing on the TV without my glasses on, and I wanted to close them and give them some rest.

Our conversation went from innocent to challenging. She said that she wanted to see me, but she couldn't get to me because the walk to my place would take too much time, besides which she wouldn't be able to stay very long. I told her not to worry; I would just borrow my stepmother's car, and we could spend more time together. I was totally bluffing and expected her to say, "No, that's okay; I know you don't have a license, so I'll just walk over for a few minutes."

Nope, she didn't say that. Instead, she JUMPED at the opportunity to sneak out and go for a ride with me. I felt this feeling in the pit of my stomach that I only got before I was going to do something stupid. It wasn't butterflies, because those are too beautiful to describe one of my bad decisions. No, what I had flying around in my stomach were moths.

I walked downstairs to the garage and looked at the Mazda parked in my stepmother's spot. Was I really going to do this? Was I going to go for a joyride—with no license, no glasses, no money, and no permission? No, I wasn't going to. This was crazy. I told myself that I couldn't do this, even as I opened the car door and saw that the keys were sitting on the seat. I got in and closed the door. Putting the key in the ignition, I just figured that I would turn it and it would not go on. There was no way. Don't cars have underage, non-license-holding locks on them? As the key turned and the engine started, I answered that question.

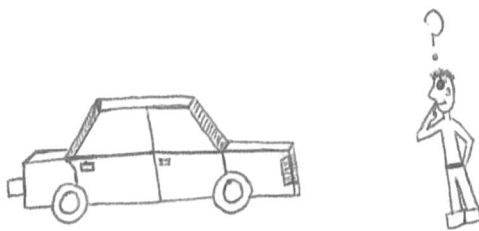

I opened the garage door with the controller and started out. The moths in my stomach were flying around faster than the ball from the movie *Flubber,* and I thought I was going to throw up. The drive was only about a mile and a half away, but it felt like an eternity. I was driving slower than shit because I couldn't really see the road.

When I got to her house, I saw her sneak out of the side door. She hopped into the car.

We didn't really go anywhere per se. We didn't park anywhere and make my current mistake an even bigger mistake. We just drove around in circles until she had to go back home. I dropped her off and headed to the gas station.

I knew where the gas gauge was when I left, so I needed to get it back to that point. After I found the gas station and filled up the gas to where I thought it was supposed to be, I headed home.

The problem with this particular situation was that my father and stepmother both *backed* their cars into the garage, and the driveway was not only long, but also sloped downward. I was going to have to drive a vehicle, with no experience, backward, down a driveway going downhill.

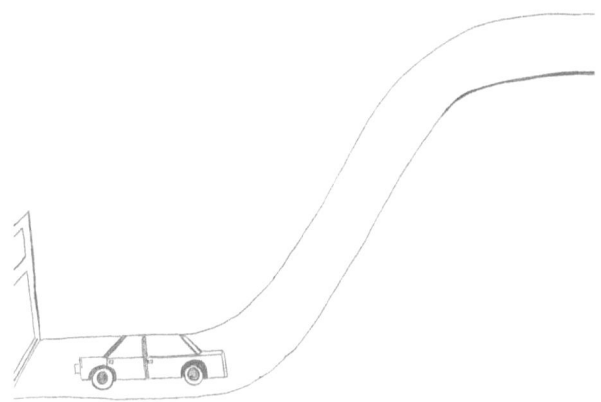

When I approached the house, I made a maneuver that I'd seen my father do before he backs down the driveway and started my descent. The front of the car went up a little, and I felt like I was going down a rollercoaster backward. I focused as hard as I could. As I neared the door, I reached up and pressed the button, waited for the door to open, and started directing the vehicle toward the garage door opening. Looking in all my mirrors, I thought I was doing a hell of a job until the car bumped forward, and I slammed on the brake. I had hit the side of the garage.

I instantly put the car in drive and pulled forward a little, readjusted, and placed the vehicle back in reverse. This time I made it into the garage.

I put the keys back where I found them in the car, opened the door, and stepped out. I looked at the side of the garage and noticed that I had left a mark. I would take care of that later. I closed the door, briefly looked over the car, didn't find anything, shrugged my shoulders, and went inside.

Aside from the mark on the side of the garage, I thought I probably got away with it and promised myself never to drive that car again.

The next day went off without a hitch. I scared myself so bad with the car situation that I spent most of the day cleaning the house and removing as much evidence of my betrayal as possible. When I took a look at the garage, I saw that the aluminum door jamb was bent a little—there wasn't much I could do about that. The door went up and down fine, so I didn't think they would notice, but I couldn't take a chance. I called up my mother's house and my stepfather answered. I spoke with him for a long time bullshitting my way back into his good graces. I told him that I wanted to come home, because I missed it there. It seemed like he genuinely wanted to help me. I picked a date, looked up the cost of plane tickets, and gave the information to my stepfather. He said they would take care of it, but I needed to be the one to tell my father.

When my dad and stepmother got home, they were very happy to see me. Hugs and kisses. Kisses and Hugs. I did the best I could to hide my guilt. They were happy, but I wasn't. They had done absolutely nothing wrong for me not to want to be there. My father, a man I looked up to so much, had no idea why I'd quit wrestling, had no idea my grades were shit, had no idea I was stealing from the neighbors, and had no idea I'd stolen the car only to crash it into the side of the house. I, on the other hand, knew all those things, and it was just a matter of time before I got caught. I needed a way out, and now I had one.

My father eventually got around to sitting me down and asking me if I'd had a chance to figure out what was making me upset, and I said yes. I blankly told him that I missed my mother, and I needed to be back in Arizona with her. He tried to reason with me, but I wouldn't budge. With every failed negotiation, my father's face grew harder. I felt like I was killing him, but I also felt that his devastation from finding out all the things that I had done would be worse. I'm not saying that I hurt my father by leaving him to protect him from the embarrassment of what I had done. I'm strong enough where I'm at in my life now, some fourteen years later, to admit that I hurt my father by leaving him because I was too much of a coward to admit my mistakes.

That would not be the last time I cowardly took the easy way out and hurt people who only wanted to take care of me.

63

WHY

Over the next week or so, the decision that I made created much tension between me and my father and stepmother. My father still showed me every day that he loved me and just wanted to see me happy. I knew he meant it, but he didn't believe that I was going to be happy in a place that I hated so much. He was right; there was no way Arizona was going to make me happy. How could it? There was nothing there that I wanted. There was nothing there worth living for, but I'd come to the conclusion that I'd rather live in a place that I feel I'm dying in, than to be in a place I liked and face my mistakes. It was time to run like I always did.

That day I told my father I was leaving him was the day I became more selfish than I ever thought I'd be. A feat that I didn't think was even remotely possible.

One night, my stepmother came into the garage where I was working out and said she wanted to talk to me. I stopped what I was doing and listened to what she was saying. She was doing her best to plead with me and beg me to reconsider. I told her I couldn't. She told me that my father was upstairs crying right then because of what I was doing to him.

My heart started to beat a mile a minute, and I wanted to scream! I wanted to tell them everything that had been happening. I wanted to tell them about the stealing and the lying. I wanted to cry and tell her that I loved them with my whole heart and just beg them for forgiveness. I didn't, however. I didn't, because I clearly didn't believe in them as much as I should have. It was my own selfishness that convinced me that they would never stand behind me and help me through this situation—so forget them.

I spent another couple of days packing my things and feeling more and more ashamed for everything that I had done. There was no turning back, and as much as I would probably hope for it in the future, I just knew that it would never happen. I would never be accepted the way I was before.

When it was time, my father was the one to drive me to the airport. We made small talk in the car, and he didn't bring up any hurt feelings. He was showing me that he would support me no matter what, and I just didn't see it at the time. I know now that I could have told him what I had done. I'm sure there would be uncomfortable consequences, but knowing what I know now, that would have been better than where I was heading.

We got to the airport, and instead of just dropping me off, he came inside and stood in line with me. He watched his son accept a ticket from the counter and act like nothing was wrong. To this day, my heart aches every time I think of that day. I should have stayed. I should have fought to be with him like he'd fought for me to be there, but I was too weak.

The plane took off, and I was on my way back to Arizona to continue on the path of mistakes that would take me down roads that you wouldn't even want to have dreams about.

I'm not going to elaborate about the plane ride home. However, I will take this time to help out people who need it besides myself.

Today I take pride in every opportunity I get to lecture parents on how they raise their kids. On paper, I have no reason to speak to them about what they're doing wrong. I have no kids and relatively no experience with them. However, what I do have is experience with me. Parents, do yourselves a favor: if you show your children day in and day out how much you love them, like my father and stepmother did, and you find yourself in a situation where they are acting differently or they want to just do something impulsive, please stand by them. But DO NOT LET THEM GO. There is clearly something wrong—and it's with them, not you. Keep them put, and get yourself an appointment with a doctor.

Kissing your kids goodnight and telling them that you love them is great, and I knowingly and wholeheartedly condone that behavior, but you can't stop there. You need to be not only a positive mentor to your children, but highly proactive in their lifestyles and decision-making. Keep your eyes open and spot the signs of trouble—and get them help early before it's too late. Help them *before* they hurt themselves.

To be continued …